SECOND CHANCE
FOR
AMERICAN PROTESTANTS

Second Chance for American Protestants

Martin E. Marty

HARPER & ROW, PUBLISHERS
NEW YORK, EVANSTON, AND LONDON

To My Brother and Sister

CONTENTS

Part Three
The Chance for the Church

PREFACE

THIS book is a radically Protestant and thus an evangelically Catholic interpretation of the Christian life in a secular culture. While I would hope that many non-Protestants, particularly of the Western Christian Church, will be moved to find parallels in their own experience, the decisive turn in the book is related to the Protestant experience. I shall argue that the first chance for evangelical witness in culture is spent, but that this is no cause for despair. The second chance, which leaves behind the assumptions of Christendom, of "placed" Christianity, permits more freedom and more mobility in the world. America, the Promised Land for Christians, then becomes America, the milieu for God's *diaspora*.

The themes in *Second Chance for American Protestants* were explored in a large number of lectures, seminars, institutes, and forums over a three- or four-year period; these occasions are too numerous to cite in this place. But this printed page provides me the opportunity of extending a second thanks to each of the hosts and all the audiences and participants. None of the material in this book has appeared earlier in printed form, at least not in exactly the way it appears here. I thank my colleague Daniel Fuelling for the refuge provided me at historic Zion Church in Bensenville, Illinois, during the period of writing, and my family for permitting me to take exile there away from children and telephones. Cecelia Gaul edited the copy and Florence Adam typed the manuscript, and I thank them, too. Finally, with this paragraph I extend gratitude to the publishers who have permitted citation from a number of books on the following pages.

MARTIN E. MARTY

Chicago, Illinois
The Last Sunday after Trinity, 1962

SECOND CHANCE
FOR
AMERICAN PROTESTANTS

1 CHRISTENDOM'S PLACE

CHRISTIANITY is an imperial power, a counter-kingdom which occupies ground.[1] So thought John Cardinal Newman, a great Christian of the nineteenth century. What he said seemed, in many ways, to be visibly true in that century. In fact, Christianity seemed to be taking what was held to be its rightful place in the world. Along with many imperial powers that were called Christian, it was conquering. It occupied specific ground. There were Christian places. There was a Christian civilization, the West. Christianity had long been mighty in certain nations. Now, in the nineteenth century, it was extending its size, going into new places in a great missionary movement. Laws were passed in its name, and hymns celebrated its power and glory among the kingdoms of men.

In the twentieth century most social and cultural forces threaten that vision of the place of Christianity. Forty years ago George Santayana[2] wrote in words that seem to be coming true: "Romantic Christendom—picturesque, passionate, unhappy episode—may be coming to an end. Such a catastrophe would be no reason for despair. Nothing lasts forever. . . ."

Ground-occupying Christendom, claiming a place under the sun, is a romantic vision. The vision—insofar as it was realized—was picturesque and passionate, though this place-inhabiting Christendom was not necessarily always unhappy. That this place-inhabiting Christendom was an episode which is coming to an end is a main theme of this book. Its end may represent a catastrophe, a violent change in all ways of looking at life. But we hope to show, with Santayana, that none of this need be a reason for despair, even in the mind and heart of the dedicated Christian.

Does Christianity need a place? The earliest events surrounding it suggest the opposite. A man who wanted to follow Jesus wherever he would go was warned that the path led to no secure settlement: "Foxes have holes, and birds of the air have nests; but the Son of man has no place to lay his head" (Luke 9:58). The earliest followers were sent out with minimum baggage: "Take nothing for your journey, no staff, nor bag, nor bread, nor money; and do not have two tunics" (Luke 9:3). Discipleship was possible without the prior existence of a Christian culture, a Christian nation or place.

The New Testament writing that bears the name of the most remembered of the disciples is conscious in its every line that Jesus' followers had no place in the occupied ground of their day. The greatest among those who were sent out into all the world reminded one of the colonies of God in an ancient city, Philippi, that their "commonwealth is in heaven" (Phil. 3:20). A nameless writer gives us the most profound parable. He pointed the early Christian communities to the record of Abraham. This father of a people was a model because "by faith [he] obeyed when he was called to go out to a place which he was to receive as an inheritance; and he went out, not knowing where he was to go. By faith he *sojourned* in the land of promise, as in a foreign land, living in tents. . . . For he looked forward to the city which has foundations, whose builder and maker is God" (Heb. 11:8-10).

The first generation of writers after the apostles addressed one another as sojourners, aliens, exiles, in the places of the era (Ignatius, Clement).[3] Most of these fathers of faith lived under the pressure and in the excitement of urgency. The time for history was short. Later, when Christians settled down for a longer stay in time and in this world, they spoke in different terms. By the

eir imperial power was
the name Christian. To
, this change represented
any modern Christians,
to the Christian genius.
an involvment in culture,
ly mission of Christians
, civilization. We by no
a largely positive view
wed the fourth century
speak of it as a passing
eed to draw on different
ggest, feel liberated and
irs of the City of Man.
go into defending Chris-
cannot participate if he
tendom.
laced Christianity?[4] We
—but by no means all
naries, evangelists, and
reveal a bondage to the
elves in constant retreat
emselves as captives of
al power receives a set-
versitles, the trade union
halls, one hears a new dirge for Christianity sung by Christians.
Many Christian scholars who strive for the place the faith deserves
among the disciplines of men cling, perhaps unswerved, to residues
of the imperial vision. The argument of this book calls not for
further retreat from the occupied ground Christianity holds, but
for a change to a different set of ground rules.

One difficulty that believers encounter in discussing the place
and the displacement of Christianity is that each holds the vision
in a way private to him. The landscape of the Western world is
dotted with the foundations of hundreds of thousands of Christian
churches. The horizon of this terrain is punctuated with countless
church towers. The temptation is to climb one's own church tower

and look around. What he sees dominates his way of thinking about Christianity.

In a place where the faith numbers many adherents and has much power, the assertion that Christianity has been displaced seems foolish and defeatist. "You never had it so good," a church extension expert reminds us as he points to the statistics of the church's numbers and finances in a few isolated parts of the world. At the other extreme, a man will climb the tall tower left over in his city from the years of Christendom and look out over the ruins of a local Christian empire. He sees other powers at work to attract or confuse men, powers that serve to empty his church and to limit his faith's claims in the world around him. To such a "church-tower historian" much of this book will seem too optimistic. I cannot claim a superior vision on the ground that my tower is higher. Rather, I must visit as many towers as possible and try to bring together the views gained from them.

A Christian reading this book, if he is an active church member in a small town or suburb where most people are Christian and churches can exercise authority in community affairs, may disagree with many of the viewpoints expressed. I would ask him to remember a world of Iron and Bamboo Curtains, of population explosions, of reawakened world religions, of competing ideologies. I would ask him to look at the inner cities to see how alien forces and hostile powers line up. A Christian reading this book, if he feels the impotence of his church in the local situation where he finds himself, may disagree with its viewpoints for the opposite reason. I would ask him to look to settings of strength. I would ask him whether his own view of past Christian strengths and opportunities may not be romantic, tinged with nostalgia.

One other preliminary difficulty: The attempt to speak of church life with an interest in the wholeness of it involves us in generalizing. It will be hard to find shorthand terms that are completely fair to the texture of reality, which is always infinitely complicated. Technical terms, which would serve best, are often barriers to understanding. This book could be regarded technically as an essay in understanding Christian life and strategy in a society which was once seen on diagrammatic lines but now is seen on dialogic lines. Once upon a time models from geography, from space, would serve. Now these static patterns will not work. The view from an airplane window suggests that the countryside men inhabit is a mosaic of field and forest, village and fortress. But the mosaic is an illusion to the earth dweller. He knows how intersectioned life is, how interrupted it is by mobility, by signals from competing value systems. New kinds of interaction and interpersonality are his experience. For shorthand reasons, I shall often speak of Christianity in the diagrammatic or spatial situation as "placed," and in the dialogic or interpersonal and intersectional situation as "displaced." I am aware of the limits of any such set of terms, but they can serve as a code or as a guide to more complex realities.

The Christian today moves in a world of displacement. The signs and signals of this reality are on every hand. When men talk about the space age, they show they are aware that the theories on the insignificant part the world as a physical unit plays in the cosmic scheme have suddenly taken on life. For centuries man has spoken of the minute place his planet holds; today this speaking is becoming a living experience. Pictures of space on the globe have changed radically. Changes in transportation and communication have brought people physically near one another. International wars have displaced empires within the places of power on the planet. The fact of genocide—the attempt to remove whole nations and peoples from the earth—is an ultimate form of displacement.

The reality of displacement has grown on man's consciousness in the presence of wandering people uprooted by war and social change. The silhouette of shuffling refugees in a thousand newsreels has informed this vision. The displaced person, the refugee, and their forty million brothers and sisters are haunting reminders that a man is no longer secure in his house. People on the move for more positive reasons in a prosperous economy are equally displaced. The "mobile home" is the residential option for millions, as it was for their tent- or cave-dwelling ancestors aeons ago. The dictator displaces people from their homes to concentration camps or to communes. The free society displaces people from their homes to promised lands. A technical society displaces people by its impersonality, its detached way of viewing and disposing them.

Most of these are not wholly new realities in human history, but quantitatively they represent a change so massive and dramatic that they produce a qualitatively new setting. A generation's common sense tells it that this change of such dimensions represents a new experience for man and his faiths. (Sometimes, as we shall see, the extent and depth of this change force men to ignore it.)

The reality of displacement is paralleled by the metaphor which points to it in literature, the arts, imaginative expression. This century's artists and poets have regularly turned to the uprooted, the detached, the dislocated, the wanderer, the stranger, the sojourner, to symbolize our times. The alien or exile gave literature its dominant motif in the past half century. The hungry refugee— the deep-set eyes, lost look, cane and shawl—is a familiar figure in representational art. Philosophy, religion, psychology, have had to deal with man's anxiety over his place in the presence of threatening weapons and forces. The need for roots and security is a constantly recurring theme.

The streams all seem to run in one direction. The physical and psychic changes that uproot men seem to be universal. Some people look to religion for islands in the streams, refuges from them. The Biblical letter to the Hebrews points to the rightful place eternity can play in providing man in the temporal world with a sane vision. This snatch at eternity is easily advertised as religion's boon to uprooted human beings. Religion is then given a place among man's hopes for the roots it offers; its stable and traditional elements are reaffirmed. In the Western world the advertised place-giving religion is Christianity.

In one sense, the promise of giving security and rootage is legitimate as a Christian claim. Christianity is rooted in place: it is an historical religion that looks to a race, land, city; a stable, hill, cross, tomb. It calls people to concrete fellowships, in a sure but temporary bond with the environment in which they find themselves. More: in its eternal dimension Christianity offers roots and grounding in the love of Christ (Eph. 3:17). Tradition plays a rightful part in Christianity, a faith which remembers and learns from the past. Tradition is attached to environment, locality—to place. To reject tradition leads to a disincarnate faith, a religion of ideas instead of interpersonality. Christianity consistently suggests certain values in withdrawal, in hiding, taking shelter from confusion, temptation, and storm. Its worship is oriented to the reality of holy places: font and altar, pulpit and prayer desk beckon people away from the crossroads. The idea of a sheltered place, a "greenhouse of the faith," can be creative in nurturing children. Disciplined church life can be symbolized in spatial terms: the Christian is in some ways separated from the world. The Christian most of all will emphathize with the man who seeks roots and place; he cannot scorn the search.

His sympathy and empathy may, however, mislead him. The temptation to engage in a false advertising of Christian claims is real. For the church to make false connections with man's desire for root and place can limit the Christian possibility—limit it in several ways, on several levels. Such limitation occurs in the discussion of learned religious scholars when they read history only conservatively. If the whole Biblical impulse to speak out against a time, to prophesy, is forgotten; if the whole sense of urgency can be denied, then Christianity can be offered to men for peace of mind, for shelter. Historians and psychologists alike often counsel the church to exploit the psychic damage that is so large a part of the debris of our time. Some among them criticize the prophets who call for an ethical or intellectual core in the Christian community; should we not rather, they suggest, be content with small-scale virtues?

People in changing cultures often desire to be undisturbed by transcultural forces. Many rebel when the church does become radical, when it speaks out about the affairs of men. The counsel then comes: The task of the churches is not to concern themselves with life in the world but to snatch people from it. Form enclaves. Gather groups of people who will turn their back on the world. Provide security.

In a short-range view of Christian destiny, these counsels appear to be wise. Temporary and isolated successes can come about when Christianity is used only to dispel creative anxieties, to sanction securities about which men should be insecure. Christians can here and there and for a moment gain the world around them and lose their own life and purpose. On the other hand, in the name of their faith and their tradition, Christians can be called to do something greatly different: to resist the temptation to exploit their historic place. When men disbelieve Christian claims but welcome Christian culture in much the same way as they welcome the security of a furnished apartment, they should be denied. Long-range Christian vision sees the limits in overidentifying with secure and often dying cultures. Christians must resist the temptation of the short-range gains that can be won by depending on a no longer vital cultural environment. Then they will experience new freedom to participate in the formation of living culture.

That sentence anticipates a possible criticism of the argument that Christians have something to look forward to in the world of increasing displacement. The argument for freedom in a dis-placing culture may look like a new appeal for individualistic culture. Or it may look like a plea for anticultural withdrawal, which could be perverted into a kind of pentecostalism that turns its back on the world. The whole task of administering the ballot box, manning the fire engine, teaching the child, producing the sculpture, leading the strike, playing the game, would then be left to non-Christians, because Christians care only for the eternal city.

Instead of for these, Christian freedom calls for new and positive relations to emerging cultures—relations entered into without ad-vance calculation as to how each of them will turn out. This posi-tion represents neither a pessimistic view of faith nor cynicism toward past custodians of Christian culture. One can take a positive attitude toward a past position, learn from it, without seeing it as the sole unfolding of history that is open today.

Most Christians live in a culture that not long ago was called "Christian" but today is described by many as "post-Christian." I prefer not to speak in these terms: in the matter of faith every age is post-Christian. But it is possible to speak of post-Christen-dom, of the erosion and breakdown of one specific Christian bond with culture; for the suffix "-dom" points to placed, ground-occupy-ing Christianity. Christendom's vital center has been displaced in the modern world. What held it together is not believed in by most of the heirs of those who fashioned it and who conquered in its name. The post-Christendom of today calls for none of the incomparable daring demanded from the exile of today who proclaimed to an unredeemed world that its redemption was here. It calls only for custodians and caretakers, curators and rear-guard defenders. The displaced Christian is free from one cultural setting only to forge a bond with another.

Even as we speak of the vital centuries of Christendom it is important not to romanticize. A Christian strategy based on the idea of imperial power, of occupying ground, tends to misrepresent history. Romantic Christendom did, as Santayana reminds us, have an unhappy aspect despite its picturesqueness. Did Christian culture so simply produce Christian faith? Did more people then believe? Did churches have things to their liking? We cannot settle these in any satisfying detail; we are more interested in seeing them in a different light. The quest for a place, however successful it may once have been, however unsuccessful it was in many ways, is not the option for Christianity today.

The early Christian is remembered in the catacomb, an alien in a pagan culture. The dedicated medieval Christian found it necessary to cloister himself in the midst of a Christian society. The pious modern Christian tended to form conventicles which turned their back on the world. Each historical phase indicates an aspect of that permanent dissatisfaction with the world that inheres in the Christian vision. What is called for in a postmodern world is neither catacomb, cloister, nor conventicle, but a real mobility and freedom to move in the middle of the world as Jesus did. As Günther Bornkamm says, he moved in this world as his home, and he moved here with an otherness that was unmistakable. The double-sidedness of his movement is a superior model for displaced Christians.

Part One

The Displacement

of Christians

2 THE ASSUMPTIONS BEHIND CHRISTENDOM'S PLACE

IN A WORLD of displacement Christianity remains as a major religion, dominant even in many areas of increasing dislocation. For centuries it has made its home in Western Europe (and, in a different form too complicated to discuss here, in Eastern Europe) and in the Anglo-American world and its outposts. It has been housed in a Christian culture, itself located inside a larger culture of waxing vitality. It has been a placed Christianity. And for the most part Christians, opposed to the idea of yielding ground, resist displacement.

The faith itself, it is held, demands a physical home, a place. It must have a geographical realm or domain, a settled if largely static bond with an environment. This insistence on ground occupation is an aspect of the Catholic way of looking at the world. The faith must have a place for the sake of its mission also. The Christian mission requires settled nerve centers, resource centers, sending centers. Before the church carries on its work of propagating the faith—so runs the argument—it needs fortresses and bastions, treasuries and strongholds. The nineteenth century, which saw the most dramatic missionary gains, developed many ways of looking at Western Europe and Anglo-America as the faith's home, from

13

which ambassadors could go out, sometimes in the name of colonial empires and usually with an interest in extending the Christian empire.

Christian nurture must have a place it can be carried on in, a protected situation of relative permanence. The gardener turns to the greenhouse when his plants are young. The warrior protects his sensitive members with armor. The church builds nurseries and seminaries (the two terms share the same intention) to shield—at least partially and temporarily—its adherents from some of the signals and symbols of rootlessness and displacement.

And, finally, Christian worship demands holy places. Men of faith build cathedrals, they revere monuments, they gaze at the tall towers of total Christendom. These cathedrals and chapels are fortresses of security, walled off from the world. Here are the historic boundaries that shut out the confusing world. Many other assumptions belong to the whole idea of placed Christianity, but in the four elements named we find the foundations of the historic reality of Christendom or Christian culture. Christendom has seen two stages: a longer (and enduring) Catholic phase and a more recent Protestant episode.* The two, though they have often been in conflict, share the axioms described above. Christendom's Catholic phase is the background of every discussion of placed Christianity. The Protestant episode has produced a different kind of defensiveness, not always culturally so visible. Isolating these defenses will be a major interest of the analytic portions of this book.

The later stage we can call Protestant*dom*. That is, it represents the identification of evangelical Christianity with a specific cultural construct in a specific place. Its specific assumptions differ from many of those in the Orthodox world of Russia, Greece, the Balkans, the ancient Near East. The Protestant empire separated itself

---

* The terms "Catholic" and "Protestant" are used here and in the pages that follow to designate distinct historic patterns of Christendom as well as definable rationalizations of these patterns. Although the terms have a reference broader than particular ecclesiastical tradition (Roman Catholics can be "Protestant" and Protestants "Catholic" in their views on Christendom), their meaning depends in considerable degree upon concepts developed and strategies employed within these traditions.

from many concerns of the Roman Catholic world, placed in southern Europe and Latin America. It never dominated on a large scale, though it may have tried and been successful in its colonies and islands, in the lands where "younger" Christian churches were born, where cultural displacement in the twentieth century has been most obvious.

From the sixteenth and down to the twentieth century, Protestantdom was one-half of the reality of Christian culture in northwest Europe, the British Isles, and—from the viewpoint of this book—most tangibly in the United States in the nineteenth century. Here was a culture formed in no small measure by evangelical Christian faith and life. Just as the Catholic looks back with nostalgia to the twelfth or thirteenth century for a model, the Protestant—usually unreflectively, I am sure—works with a myth of a paradisiacal golden age in sixteenth-century Europe and nineteenth-century America. In this mythology the cultural, missionary, educational, and liturgical possibilities were in proper sequence and array. (That much of the picture *is* mythical is not important here; myth may be more formative and overpowering than history!)

Christendom and Protestantdom represent not only axioms and attitudes but a specific substance or content. Again, it seems unjust to condense so much variety into a few assertions, but this can be done fairly and briefly for our purpose.

Such "placed" Christianity implies a historical pre-emption of an environment. The non-Christian may be tolerated or even welcomed, but he is the stranger and the guest. He may be allowed religious freedom, but this freedom is usually argued for on lines which are presumed to be specifically Christian. "This is *our* home, and you are welcome." Christendom demands not only this historic lease on the environment, this sense of the furnished apartment. It seeks also a contemporary status and respect. The furniture is to be admired by the stranger or the guest for its present—not merely its historical—function and beauty. Placed Christianity looks after its prerogatives and endowments, its treasure and its good name, its walls and its towers.

Christendom and Protestantdom look for at least four other kinds of ties to culture. Historically dominant was the *legal* tie.

The laws of men were to be informed by the Law of God, often as dispensed by the church as its custodian. The administration of law, the execution of justice, was usually seen to be a mutual task of what today we call church and state. The forms of this legal tie changed constantly. In the Middle Ages it was often personified by the conflicts and co-operations of Pope and Emperor. The legislator, it was implied, consulted the church or represented the church. Protestantism rejected much of the medieval understanding, but its own culture produced new forms of the same reality.

Thus in the nineteenth century American Protestants, who were officially legally disestablished, represented the kinds of power blocs and suasions which could produce laws that helped Protestant claims take life. Many of the antibirth-control, antigambling, Sunday-closing, and prohibition laws of the nineteenth and twentieth centuries are residues of the attempt legally to impose a Protestant view of morality on a larger community which shared only some aspects of Protestant culture.

Christendom looked also for *ideological* ties to culture. These ties were never so simple and direct as they may appear to us today. Pope and Emperor, church patron and artist, Christian university and philosopher, were very rarely in sympathy in such ways that real concordats or syntheses could be worked out. Yet when Christianity really had a place in the world, representatives of the host culture ordinarily would place the adjective "Christian" in front of their enterprises. Most attempts to isolate, codify, and reproduce the details of these ideologies are unfair and embarrassing. But in the thicket of detail, in the many strands of philosophy at which we still pull, there is a main branch or major skein of assumptions about culture that has at least diffuse origins in Christian claims. A "Christian philosophy" of culture was sought and maintained.

The *moral* tie was a corollary of the other two. It became dominant when the others—legal and ideological—began to weaken. In America legal disestablishment came early in the life of the nation (the First Amendment to the Constitution) and quite early (1774 to 1833 or 1834) in the life of the states. The Anglo-American world has not been particularly adept at fashioning ideologies. So the legal-ideological vacuum was filled by a moral and sometimes moralist impulse. The Christian and (in the United States at least) Protestant views of morality made their way through persuasion and through social forms of coercion that were much more subtle than formal law. The mores of a nation can tyrannize as well as the laws; it can also shape the positive aspects of living.

Finally, a _cultural_ tie, in the production of art and artifact, was assumed. This tie was more prominent in the Catholic phase than in the Protestant episode of placed Christianity for many reasons. Bach, Milton, Rembrandt, Melville, are names that can symbolize these cultural ties in four places, times, phases of evangelical culture, and in four media of expression. Much of the subject matter and even more of the stance of cultural representatives such as these is informed by a relation to the Christian faith and an understanding of their own environment.

At least these four elements are implied in any discussion of the historic realities of Christian culture and their incarnation in any specific place.

In colloquial terms, each means that the cards of history are stacked in favor of the church or of Christian claims; the fabric of a time is made up in no small part of Christian thread. In moments when such a fusion or interaction is vital and alive it needs little defense (twelfth-century Europe, nineteenth-century America). When the place of Christianity is insecure, when its cultural house is attacked, defense tends to become strident and panicky (early sixteenth-century Europe, mid-twentieth-century America).

If it is important to know the axioms and realities of placed Christianity, it is equally important to learn what defenders of the culture it produces fear as alternatives to it. Sometimes these fears are articulated (Christopher Dawson, Jacques Maritain, T. S. Eliot, are Catholic examples of sophisticated defense of Christian culture); just as often they belong to folk expression and appear to be unconscious.

One of these feared alternatives is that Christendom and even the Christian faith will be supplanted, displaced, engulfed, and eventually obliterated by later, larger, more vital or coercive cultures.

Christians do not often use the sword (Middle Ages) or the ballot box (nineteenth century) to enforce their claims; they no longer have the power to. But other cultures can be totalitarian in their claims. To raise questions about placed Christianity causes concern lest Christians yield ground, give up their place under the sun, to tyrannies, competing cultures, or even anticultures and destructive spirits. These opponents may be formal ideologies, such as Communism; or pervasive ways of looking at life, such as the scientific world view; or inclusive ways of living life, such as we see in a technical society.

Another fear, already referred to, is that if Christians do not defend the specific cultures which are in part their own creation, they may lose interest in carrying cultural burdens. The Christian response in a world of bewildering displacement may be one of reaction and withdrawal. Christopher Dawson scores Protestants for rejecting the idea of a Christian civilization.[1] He remarks that "the school of existentialist neo-Kierkegaardian Christianity" which has had such an influence on the religious intelligentsia fosters such a rejection.

Refusal to be culturally involved, anticultural attitudes, or rejection of the cultural impact of Christianity are not, however, the only alternatives to the "Christian civilization" which Dawson defends.

Sometimes Christian withdrawal is temporarily necessary. Behind the Iron Curtain, Christians are sometimes given the choice between a martyrdom that may *not* provide blood for the seed of the church (modern totalitarianisms are too efficient, too secretive!) and a living but "noncultural" witness. No small measure of the Christian thought which trickles out from under the rusty base of the Iron Curtain seems to be evidence that existentialist and individualist Christianity, "saving souls" or merely enduring, is often the only form of expression possible. The free world in its luxury is in poor position to provide Christian judges for that form of witness. But as concerns the free world Dawson is correct: anticultural attitudes could easily be an irresponsible form of reaction if once Christendom—placed Christianity—were supplanted.

A third fear of defenders of ground-occupying Christendom is that Christians may develop abstract forms of expressing faith. The heresy which snatches Christianity from its bonds with environments, its dialogue with persons, its connections with cultures, remains attractive. At the least the Christian forms of faith that demanded a place under the sun were daily reminders of the concrete character of life. Children played in the streets, couples danced at weddings, buildings were built and occupied, calluses were formed, nuts and bolts sorted, systems of philosophy written, furnaces stoked—and it was to this world that the Christian faith responsibly addressed itself. Were an unhistorical, spiritualistic (Docetic) Christianity the alternative, we would need bell ringers calling people back to the tall towers of total, romantic Christendom.

A last cultural alternative that defenders of Christendom fear is this: Without a place of Christian culture, will there not be a diffusion of people's identities? How will I know who I am and where I belong if I am a man of faith living in a complex and competitive culture? Can I develop character, a view of life, a cultural expression, without an environment in which I really feel at home? This is a dramatic problem for young people in a pluralistic culture. Few of the signals provided them in the nurtured setting of their early years remain clear once they go out into the open, signal-jamming environment. Will there not be corrosion and erosion that wear away not only at my place in society, but at me? At my faith? This subtlest anxiety has the most warrant of all, and for it there are no easy solutions. A preliminary reply would be: It is at least preferable to live without illusions and masks. As far as possible, one's faith should make its way in a real world and not in a masquerade or puppet show. Attempts to change and improve culture must be made within the context of the possibilities. Pumping new life into a corpse, advertising the unexciting in the name of Christianity, is not a creative strategy. The problem of the diffusion of identity must be dealt with in other, more realistic ways.

We have looked at the positive elements in the axioms of placed Christianity and at the negatives of fear that haunt its defenders.

Remembering these will help explain the characteristic modes of thinking and the tactics which the defenders employ. Usually they are reduced to retreat, to holding operations, to yielding each year as little ground as necessary for Christendom to remain plausible. At their hands, Christians are made to appear cautious and conservative caretakers of a museum that few care to visit. Christians may seek to regain or reclaim lost territory and, here and there, to extend the Christian place. Most often they must content themselves with finding partial solutions on spatial models.

In the nineteenth century men of goodwill in the United States formed a colony and a government in West Africa called Liberia. It represented an attempt at a diagrammatic solution. The displaced Negro, freed from slavery, would be returned to his place, his culture. By this solution the slave-owning, oppressive white would be free to act and look Christian again, the temptation to exploit another human would be removed from his environment. But little was done to deal with the interpersonal majority who came face to face with whites at the intersections of urban life in North and South.

In the twentieth century men of goodwill, using a spatial model, try again to rectify an evil racial situation. In the face of segregation in the cities they seek to break down the absoluteness of the barriers between white and Negro communities. Knowing that in the present economic pattern the barriers are usually broken violently in community change, they conceive an ingenious plan based on the idea of place: a quota system, through which, it is agreed, a number of nonwhites will be permitted to live on a particular block. Promises are made that this move will represent a limit so that property values will remain where they are. Here again the motives may be good. But the artificiality, the temporal and even exploitative character of this condescending attempt soon became patent. The essence of a modern free society is its interpersonal or intersectional possibility; a Liberia, a quota system, are static, implicitly coercive settlements based on assumptions as to place.

To use a religious illustration: American Roman Catholics ordinarily believe something different concerning the means of limiting births than do their Protestant, Jewish, and nonreligious neighbors. Most social studies reveal that while their beliefs differ, their practices are often alarmingly (from their church's point of view) similar. Catholics, displaced in a competitive and varied culture, experience the jamming of signals and diffusion of identities discussed above. A responsible Roman Catholic leader proposed a solution based on the model of place. Catholics should form "open ghettos." Without breaking off commercial or civil contact, they should disrupt the relative intimacy in which personal values are discussed and shared with these non-Catholics. Again, the limitations of such a suggestion become immediately apparent. It represents a defensive, partial, and artificial solution.

These solutions based on wall, ghetto, ward, sector, colony— diagrammatic models all of them—provide a background for understanding the thought and action of defenders of placed Christianity. Their action takes many forms. Ordinarily it will reveal an instinctive regard for the European or American environments. This is natural; there is no place like home. But the value judgments which are marks of loyalty to the familiar are easily perverted into ideologies which confuse Christian claims. Recently numbers of conservative statesmen and editorialists in Europe and America have argued that the West is God's civilization. The implication is that if the West changes, declines, or "goes under," God has run out of possibilities. The Euro-American myopia may blind Christians to a new destiny for their faith in a time when the European-American unfolding of Christianity should be remembered for what it was: a moment, an episode, an instant in the history of man.

Within the Euro-American defense pattern, more often than not Christianity will be tied to the more reactionary and self-preservative elements in that culture. A Tory view of life is somehow compatible with the belief that Christian civilization provides the least revolutionary laws and ideologies, the surest forces, the most gentlemanly manners. In a revolutionary world low expectations are brought to such preservations and the long-range missionary possibility of this quietly imperialist view is limited.

Christian defensiveness also leads to an instinctive and often unconscious alliance with the generalized religiousness and religiosity of a culture. Such an alliance, it is assumed, will provide coherence and protection, a buffer against the world, against the confusions of secularity. What is not often observed is the variety of competing and confusing signals under the overarching tent of religiousness. That the religious man, whose hands are full of his own claims and righteousnesses and pieties, is less open to Christian discipleship than is the world-oriented neighbor ought to be clear from any reading of the Gospels. Jesus had more success with Mary Magdalene, Zacchaeus, and the "people across the tracks" than he did with the representatives of religion.

Insistence on the "rights" of Christian culture and the churches, without the ability to carry out sanctions against opponents, further places defenders of Christendom in a retreating position. When Christian claims are presented arrogantly in legal or judicial chambers, in art galleries or lecture halls, this insistence on the churches' prerogatives and good name is implied. But the church, impressive as its power blocs may be, lacks the sword or the jailbars—and, often, even the social pressure—to enforce its claims. When the vote, the decision, the expression, goes against Christianity another pathetic weakness of the church has been revealed. The larger society is in a position to exploit these weaknesses.

Still other defenders of the Christian place are given to erratic forms of resistance to threats. Maginot lines, fortresses of the faith, are erected. The church becomes a willing partner with all other elements in society that resist revolution, rightly or wrongly. In the United States this fortress-and-hand-grenade approach to Christian defense is frequently apparent in forms of resistance to the depiction of our society as pluralistic. By "pluralistic" we mean only that many fonts of religion and values flow, many kinds of signals are free possibilities. This should be the first visible fact about life in the New World, but many Christians still advocate "Christian Amendments to the Constitution"[2] and do what they can to create the illusion that the adjective "Christian" can and should apply to all elements of culture.

Most of these forms of defensiveness force their advocates to focus on the institutional self-preservation of churches. Build strongholds of the faith in the suburban islands, erect new tall towers, advertise the institution's merits, look to its endowments! At the same time, as often as not, there is little reckless and self-abandoning expenditure of the ecclesiastical hoards on either the mission of the church or its service of the world.

Finally, the view that Christianity must occupy ground leads to reluctance to face the world religions and ideologies on mission fields in open dialogue. Again, the intentions of defensive Christians are or may be good. One seeks to carry on a mission to an unbelieving world. An unexposed faith can more easily be presented in the form of capsules and formulas. The world will yield its few to the mission. What is not often noticed is the by-product of this curious reluctance to expose the faith in risk. Not only in areas of mission but also at the sending centers people draw the conclusion that Christianity is a provincial faith, dependent entirely on a certain constellation of cultural factors. It is afraid to be open where these factors are not all present.

In subsequent chapters we shall have to ask whether the forces which displace Christians from their cultural home are reversible. Do any signs exist to tell us that the drift and movement of history are in the direction away from displacement? Will there again be occupied ground, a place under the sun? Will the cards be stacked in the churches' favor in new ways?

At this point it should be made clear that our focus is not on faith but on culture. We are not suggesting—though the reader may have opinions—that it is either easier or harder to believe in one age than in another. The displaced Christian is not necessarily nearer to either faith or to unbelief than his settled ancestor, or than his nervous contemporary who is custodian of the monuments of Christendom. Nor is one simple force doing the displacing. To speak of displaced Protestantism does not mean that Catholicism will prevail; of displaced Christianity, that Judaism will prevail; of displaced Biblical religion, that other religions of a specific character will prevail. Each of the religions makes its way. They and secularism, religiousness, casual practical unbelief, fascination with pluralism—

all may be resurgent. A cluster of forces whose net effect is "secularity" characterizes the world of displaced Christendom. That concept must be kept as neutral as possible for the present. A combination of religious and nonreligious interpretations of life complicates Christian cultural self-seeking.

3 THE ASSAULT ON
CHRISTENDOM'S PLACE

How do Christians become conscious of threats to the security of their place? What are the mechanisms by which these threats relate themselves to Christianity? Has secularity a stance and a content? Both the formal (sociological) and the material (ideological) questions must be dealt with.

Formally, the relations of the larger world to the residue of Christendom are different in kind as well as in degree from those of the past. Understanding of this formal distinction can be an aid to Christians in their strategy. Shall they choose to permit exposure to social and cultural change? Or shall they, wherever possible, create barriers against contact and influence?

The essence of modernity is the change from life on a diagrammed or spatial, sectioned model to life as a dialogical, dynamic, intersectioned reality.[1] The term "dialogic" as over against "diagrammatic" requires a little analysis. In a mass society, there may be more interaction but there is not necessarily more real interpersonality than in the earlier model. By intersectioned I mean something as simple as what happens at crossroads. Many kinds of signals and contacts are present and influential; no value judgment as to the depth of personal contact in the criss-crossing is presented.

But *some* kinds of signals do "come through" to jostle those that the previously isolated people brought to the crossroads. The static, isolated, "placed" view is not necessarily inferior; it has its obvious virtues and they carry their nostalgic appeal. Recall of the valleys of tradition, the wards and sectors and ghettos of family and clan life, finds us looking at old pages in family albums and warmly remembering. Aspects of these values can be nurtured in the midst of modernity. But as a basic, undergirding view of life, any thought or strategy founded on this picture is living on borrowed time with limited resource.

Ordinarily the only effective way to avoid or counter forces of dialogue, interpersonality, intersectionality, is through coercion. Yet even the forced disruption of dialogue issues in displacement. The Nazi "nurseries" and concentration camps, the Soviet prisons and Siberian exiles, the Red Chinese antheap communes, are solutions along the lines of coercion and place, but dislocation is the profound effect. Yet it is in the coerced society that the most effective defenses against the new model are made. Iron and Bamboo Curtains, the jamming of "Voice of America" radio signals, segregation of races—all these are tangible symbols of the way only the coercive society is really successful at resisting intersectioned, interpersonal life. The secretive efficiency of a totalitarian state is another example. But a free society permits relative freedom of movement. A world without walls is the effect of a free society's openness.

What aspects of displacement most serve to crowd or jostle Christendom's settlement? Most massive is the population explosion, a decisive counter to any claim that the ground Christians occupy or the place under the sun they hold is growing or can easily grow. Picture the most intensive increase in Christian missionary activity possible in the context of present-day resources; it could not begin to reverse the current trend of movement away from Christian claims. We must linger here for a moment. Despite our inability to deal with staggering statistical change, we cannot use this as an excuse to relegate the fact of population growth to the quieter portions of our imagination. Instead, it may be profitable to take an instance of Christian strategy based on a sense of place and claim and see it in the light of population development.

A denominational church extension tract, rooted in diagrammatic thinking as such tracts usually are, appeals for missionary prayers and resources. It uses what public-relations experts call "the bandwagon effect." Psychologically its appeal suggests: "We are winning. We are almost 'over the top.' Join us now, before it is too late. Give a bit more to the cause. We can then wipe out the last pockets of resistance." The tract then asks one to choose its denomination for support because of that denomination's statistical success. It is one of the fastest-growing groups in the United States. In only twenty-five years it has grown from, say, 1.5 million to 2.5 million nominal adherents (fill in the figures of your choice). This looks like a startling gain. Whoever rejoices in the inclusion of one lost sheep, lost coin, lost son, knows that "there is joy in heaven" over each.

But the appeal of the tract is based entirely on illusion. What was the world doing in the twenty-five years during which the denomination added one million? In the week the tract was being printed the world added *two* million babies to its population. Of course, the denomination in question, while it could boast of its fast growth, was not doing the whole work of the church. It represents, one might estimate, about 1/350th of the whole of nominal Christianhood in the world. Suppose the whole church were successful in the same statistical degree multiplied by 350; still, no extension of Christian territory would be implied. Those who point to America's size and dominance in the world and who take comfort from its Christian place and predominance are less sanguine when reminded that in the last four years alone the whole world has grown by the United States' present population.

We can picture a graph:[2] Let each little manlike figure on it represent 100 million people. Suppose the world population grew (actually it could not) at its present pace, with the same curve of the graph, from A.D. 1950 to 2050. North America's "two little men" (200 million) would become six (600 million). If the Christian impact continues in America, well and good for its future place under the sun. How does this fit in the rest of the world? Europe, where Christianity is in a more complex setting, as of now is represented by four "little men"; in a century it would have eight. Soviet Russia would grow from two to eight; Africa (or Latin America) from about two to thirteen; Asia, where the Christian place under the sun hardly casts a shadow, would grow from fourteen such figures (1.4 billion) to 108 (10.8 billion).

Population growth is important, of course, not only for the world's statistical picture but also for what crowding does to the idea of open space for retreat and shelter. The American "son of the middle border" on the frontier a century ago could report that, when an undesirable neighbor moved in, his family easily solved the problem: they could pack up and move to the next grove, brook, or pasture and strike out anew. A crowding world knows no place to hide (though urban refugees in the finer suburbs still create the illusion that there may be!). While mere proximity, we suggested, is not enough for real interpersonality, a crowding society does emit and receive certain kinds of transcommunal symbols. Christianity's place will be complicated by these.

Mobility is the second apparently permanent social factor that must be reckoned with. Here again the statistics must be personified and made vivid. The *Völkerwanderungen,* the wanderings of exiled, refugee, displaced peoples in our time, dwarf all earlier processions. The tenant farmer, share-cropper, and "Okie" of the American thirties revealed that nomadism is a necessary part of life in a time of economic depression. One must go to the oases, the resource centers, to work, eat, or receive handouts. In prosperity the situation is merely intensified. A technical society prepares man for a specific task in a complicated, national operation. As he completes the task, he moves. As he rises (or falls) on the economic scale, the average American is said to move every five years. Christian ministers on college campuses sometimes complain of their congregations' mobility: "We only have our members for four years." The suburban minister replies: "If only we had ours for four years!" Nomadism is not new, of course. But today's wandering differs substantially from that of the past in that today's wanderer does not travel with the same people, with tribe or clan. He comes into contact with wholly new groups of equally rootless and restless people and their values.

Such mobility is no cause for simple pessimism. It has possibilities for culture and for the Christian faith. But it represents significant change. Historic Christian nurture in the "placed" setting of the parish was based on the idea of a years-long if not life-long contact with a family and a community of Christians. Mobile people tend to take less responsibility for their environment; they tend to develop different patterns of loyalty. Who can picture loyalty to a mass-produced modern suburb; or at least, who can picture such a loyalty that must not be equipped to change allegiance patterns regularly? Further, mobility represents displacement, jostling, intimate contact with people of other value systems. The shelter and protection afforded by one's own value system are removed. Parsons and religious strategists who yearn for the return of the "good old days" of normal parish life (on the pattern of static place) are not dealing realistically with life in a technical, crowding society.

Another and in some respects most decisive displacing interruption is the modern system of mass communications. A man's home may be his castle, but it is threatened by the fact that today it has subtle, relatively quiet infiltrators in the form of books, magazines, newspapers, radio, television, and other communications media. These are decisive in that they bring the impact of all other social forces to bear on one's consciousness. People derive no small portion of their view of reality from these media. To assume that Christian nurture and evangelism can proceed without interruption or disruption in the face of these forces is unrealistic.

Urbanism, which is in part a product of the other factors, is another fact which jostles the picture of a Christian imperium. The city in history may once have meant civility, the home of order and pattern and civilization. In the modern world it may mean this; it may also mean the presence of chaos, of the barbarian. The cities, reminds Rilke, play us false and are beguiling alike to beasts and infants. Modern urbanism has developed a new and separate kind of spirit. Its modes of determining truth and value, its means of exercising power, contradict most of those developed in the long years of Christendom. The modern metropolis is the home of population crowding, mobility, the mass media. The future belongs, for better or for worse, to the city and the urban mentality.

All this does not, again, imply real interpersonality. Arnold Bennett when he viewed the American cities observed that the very architecture seemed to breathe humanity but that men were very much alone. Yet the city develops intersectionality. The subway conversation, the newspaper headline, the sport or entertainment world, the political campaign, the advertising slogan, the crowd, represent kinds of intersectional life with which securely placed Christendom cannot well reckon.

Last, we might cite a cluster of other disturbances which serve to displace. Modern war, the ultimate conflict with its demands for unconditional surrender, represents disruptions of civilian life unheard of in previous centuries. The political boundaries change, causing new "Christian-non-Christian" configurations. (Think of the religious implications of the division at a conference table—without consultation with the citizens involved—of the map of Germany into an Eastern and a Western part.) Racial or religious intermarriage, military service, the uprooting in the modern public school, and college experience are domestic examples. On the world-wide scale almost every instance of new nationalism and anticolonialism—one of the most dramatic of forces in the world today—reflects against a Christian imperium or culture.

No place to hide—this has been the theme. Islands are fewer, unjammed signals rare. Christianity does not today have (and does not ordinarily desire) the totalitarian tools necessary to coerce a static sense of place, to defend its territory. Defenses based on suasion and rhetoric are seldom heeded. Only new kinds of relations to emerging cultures can hold possibilities for the future.

If the formal principle of modernity is the jostling of people, the criss-crossing of value systems, its material base must also be considered, however briefly. What is the substance, the net effect, of the content of these jostling realities? One can be specific and say that at different places in the world different jostlers are at work. In many former missionary strongholds which were the result of sending centers in the nineteenth-century imperium of Christendom, some of these specific signals can be isolated easily. Mohammedanism, Buddhism, Hinduism, Communism, may be cited. Reborn world religions, largely quiescent in the nineteenth century when Christians took their territories by surprise, must now be reckoned with as complicators. (Needless to say, the entrance into the modern or postmodern world of most of the once-isolated regions where these religions predominate represents the same kinds of challenges to their religious cultures that the West has been experiencing.)

Overarching, undergirding, and accompanying these reborn religions or aggressive ideologies and political idolatries is another reality which seems to be the inevitable corollary of modern life. It reaches into the conscious and unconscious life and decision of the people who occupy the terrains of each world religion. It seems to come as a partner to technical and scientific life, a cousin to pluralism. This reality can be called by the neutral term "secularity" (as opposed to secularism)—a way of looking at life which is nonreligious in the ordinary sense of the term. This way of viewing life is so pervasive that it can absorb religious views of life in their decisive aspects. It can even spawn a religious sense which in some subjective way serves to feed secularity.

The birth of the modern world and its pluralism led to the conception of this secularity. It is the basic substantive fact of modern life in the portions of the world called Christian or post-Christian or non-Christian. It affects fundamentalists and modernists, disciplined and relaxed adherents of all religions and of no religions. To picture someone completely exempt from its influence is to picture the hermit—and even he is influenced by what he negates. The world religions and particularly the Christian faith will have to deal with this form of modern consciousness if they wish to relate to the future.

Some historians find it necessary to speak in dramatic terms of "the death of God" as the fact at the base of today's society.[3] This more sweeping terminology may be accurate, but we refrain from using it here for fear of alienating those who may follow the argument if it is consonant with their own observations concerning modern spiritual and social life. Secularity finds its point of reference in an assumption quite different from one which gave the impetus to Christendom. The assumption is that whether or not God exists (and he very well may, and may very well be served

in traditional ways) is not of decisive importance in human affairs.
A British Christian apologist, Eugene Rolfe,[4] observes that in
most of the significant decisions of life all of us reveal that it is
not important to us whether or not God exists. At this point we
shall not suggest what this observation means for Christian theology,
except for saying that it means change in interpretation of culture.
The "all of us" of Rolfe's comment might actually be very much
at home with one set of Biblical resources.

We consult the weatherman instead of God to learn meteorology.
In so doing we may be more in accordance with the Biblical as-
sertation that God lets his sun and rain fall on the evil and good
alike than are those who look for supernatural intervention to as-
sure rain on their crops or sun on their Sunday School picnic. A
different kind of sign, Jesus reminded, was sought in his kingdom.
The modern political state, drenched in the kind of secularity that
can use or not use the name of God to similar effects, may be
near some New Testament pictures. It may have more to do with
Jesus' attitude toward Jerusalem and Rome, more to do with Romans 13 and I Peter, than did the Holy Roman Empire or the
Protestant establishments of New England. That question need
not be settled here. But pervasive secularity at the root of decision
for religious and nonreligious alike must be reckoned with.

The process of seeing the world on its own natural terms has
been unfolding in new ways for four and a half centuries. Chrono-
logically, the tendency has been to displace views thought to be
Christian, beginning from the most remote (outer space) to the
most near (inner man). In popular thought, in piety, the first displacement is still the most profound and still affects discussion of
Christian thought. The recent debates over the removal of mythic
strands in the Biblical world view reflect an interest in this difficulty of man in recent centuries to locate himself.

Without doubt most of the assumptions behind Christendom
assigned a central place in the universe to the ground Christians
occupied. Out of the richness of Biblical witness to the greatness of
the whole creation (see Job 38 and 39) those elements were chosen
which placed man's world in the center. The stars punctured the
dark firmament, the sun was a fiery ball in the heavens, the win-

dows of heaven opened when it rained, heaven was up and hell was
down. Not that either the Biblical witness or Christian thought was
ever so unsophisticated. But popular preaching and piety worked
with such a universe. In it, God was always behind the process or
beyond it. Remove the curtain of man's current horizon or boundary of ignorance and God would be found there.

When science was introduced in the Copernican revolution and
the world of man was displaced to be seen as spatially insignificant,
many forms of modern unbelief were born. If God was not "out
there," where was he? Each time he was assigned a location behind a nether curtain of man's current ignorance he failed to
appear when the curtain was withdrawn. Each time he served as
the x in a year's equations he failed to stand up when the new
year's $Q.E.D.$'s were written. In the move from the closed world
to the infinite universe, God was edged out and the agony of
modern unbelief was born. That God's transcendence was not
necessarily conceived of in spatial terms was a salutary reminder
disregarded by those whose habit of mind had located him "out
there." That the new view of space (whose assumptions are
only now beginning to be lived out) may enlarge the range of
human possibilities was lost on an embarrassed church. Its decisive claim—that it knew the whereabouts of God (as common
people thought)—was undercut. The world was maturing; Christendom was beginning to be displaced in the thought patterns of
the world. Anyone who ministers to a campus generation that has
had its first bout with the scientific world view—and compares it
with Sunday School lessons; anyone who ministers to a pious
family—if it has not been particularly informed by the full Biblical
witness—at the time of a death, will agree that this first assault
is still the most devastating.

Each of the later steps in the process can be seen to be moving
nearer the center of man's existence. Human use of space is best
perceived in the socio-political sphere. Here the second phase
of formal secularity was lived out in the Christian West. It was in
America, in the New World, toward the end of the eighteenth
century, that the great secular revolution in directing the state
occurred. This revolution was most decisive in bringing about the

disintegration of Christendom. It reveals the true nature of secularity. The disestablishment of the churches, the relative separation of church and state, the beginnings of voluntaryism, have been variously interpreted. They can be seen as mere practical solutions to the problem of competing religions in a modern state. They can be seen as what they often were—concessions in the name of natural religion, or "Nature's God," a deity that did not offend the religious. On the other hand, they can be seen as the work of atheists and enemies of the church. And, on the extreme other hand, the whole process can be claimed as authorized by the church. Protestants of all stripes and Catholics of many now scramble to take credit for this change in the political order— even though most of them were dragged reluctantly into it.

The new secularity in politics suggests the degree to which religiousness and nonreligiousness are irrelevant to the question of concrete public decision. Ever since, in a pluralist society, political prayers have been noted for their generally vacuous character. The gods prayed to in the name of a national interest tend to cancel one another out or to be so bland and impotent as not to be able to do even that. In any case, the human auditors do not really expect anything decisively different to occur because of the prayer. It is a form to be gone through. Equally important to the modern church is the liberating potential in certain forms of secularity. Few Protestants, at least, would like to go back to the formal, legal bases of placed Christianity—though many of them still desire an informal, semilegal status for it.

Closer and closer to individual man the concentrics of secularity have moved. In historiography, men's conception of the world moved from supernature to nature, from providence to progress to process, from deity to purpose to mere empirics. In philosophy, the movement was from metaphysics to physics to analysis as to how truth is expressed. The subject matter of art was decisively secularized. While the art of the West from the fourth to the sixteenth century concentrated on Christian themes, the modern gallery of art presents a minute percentage of work recalling Christian themes and myths. The assumptions of education changed. The child was not to be indoctrinated with truths that came from "beyond"; he was to be educated: something latent (which could hardly be, in classic terms, the content of a revealed religion) would be led out of him. Each of these transitions was largely accepted by Christian and non-Christian alike, acceptance or rejection apparently having little to do with how life is lived. The later changes were, once again, more dramatic. Within the last century the Darwinian revolution, locating itself in the question of man's origins, jostled man's sense of uniqueness in his Christian place. The Freudian impetus asked questions of the distinctiveness of the inner spirit of man quite different from the questions asked in the light of classic Christian concerns.

Some of the agents of change were god killers. Others were dedicated Christians, convinced that they were fulfilling the Biblical command to subdue and dominate the creation. Some changes were received with panic and others with apathy. To some the churches accommodated, against others they at first rebelled. In the end each change was somehow incorporated into Christian consciousness without apparently calling for many adjustments in the actual decisions of life.

"In the fight between you and the world, back the world." Does the advice of Kafka apply here? Should the religious man, engaged in recurrent retreat in the name of his disappearing gods, abandon his belief and congratulate secularism? Or are there potentials for him, if he is freed of his defensive attitudes, in asserting the Lordship of Christ at the centers of a casual world? He has seen many of the once vital structures of Christendom reduced to skeletons. Skeletons, it is true, invite inquiry, and he may amuse for a time by speculating concerning their historic meaning.

He must, however, ask seriously whether he may not do better service to his God by abandoning the whole retreat and the rules of its game. Must he be only the antiquarian, the caretaker of skeletons shuffling through the museums of his passing civilization? Or is there an honest Christian way to win freedom from the burden of advertising his virtues in cultural and social life?

Where the form of secularity we have described will go, we cannot speculate. The future of belief and the future of unbelief are both in doubt. Does the fact that secularity breeds a spirit of subjective and generalized religiousness suggest that man is incurably religious? That the world will remain adolescent, dependent upon the gods? Must the believer, seeing his interest in a divine base of objective phenomena undercut, content himself with interest in the religious subject? Does the Enemy of the good in the City of Man have anything to fear from religions that concentrate only on man in the act of being religious? These are important questions for the future of faith. They are vital here only for their part in the cultural issue before us.

As Christendom faces the world today, secularity has a prior claim over Christian and non-Christian alike in their practical decisions. God becomes, in Bishop Stephen Bayne's apt term, an optional God. He may exist; he may not. No matter, affairs go on the same either way. The dedicated Christian believer, to the degree that he is involved in culture, knows that he represents a partial culture inside a whole culture and that this fact has decisive impact on his understanding of life.

The whole culture and the partial culture: How do these relate? Where is the vitality located? This book celebrates the vitality of Christian faith and the comatose state of historic Christian cultures. Custodianship of the latter may well limit the life of the former. Observe the dynamism of Christian antiquarians and the museum-keepers, of cautious Christian artisans and timid Christian thinkers, and compare them to workers in the visceral, pulsing, competitive world of arts, labor, revolution, politics, entertainment, even on their most banal levels—and it is not difficult to see on what side many in society would cast their vote.

A parable that comes to my mind too frequently for comfort (though it was told with a different intention) is Franz Kafka's story "The Hunger Artist."[5] The hunger artist lived in a time when people, instead of watching marathon dancing or six-day bicycle racing, paid money to watch a man fast. He occupied a small cage placed in the village center. He could go forty days without food. People would come daily to watch his performance, to wonder at his ability to cling to life. Some would arrange for season passes. Eventually the human's capacity for being bored by even the most agonizing performances won out. Fascination turned to boredom and boredom turned to rejection. People were repelled by the sight of the man.

In the end the hunger artist is reduced to joining a carnival. His cage is placed along the passage to the animals, so that passers-by still note him passingly. Among the animals is a panther, young and alert. Crowds gather around it. In the great cat people see new vitality and excitement, the will to live (not merely to endure) and to conquer. The artist appears more repulsive than ever. At his death he confesses. Why did he choose this line of work, this perverse form of entertainment? He fasted, he said, because "I could not find the food I liked." Compare the cat, stalking his domain: "The food he liked was brought to him without hesitation by the attendants; he seemed not even to miss his freedom; his noble body, furnished almost to the bursting point with all it needed, seemed to carry freedom around with it too; somewhere in his jaws it seemed to lurk; and the joy of life streamed with such ardent passion from his throat that for the onlookers it was not easy to stand the shock of it. But they braced themselves, crowded round the cage, and did not want to move away."

In my remythologizing of this parable, the residue of settled, placed Christendom is *not* represented by the panther. Not all details of any parable should be pressed all the way, and I would not like to see this one carried too far. But one line should be introduced: the panther—read: the world displaced from Christian moorings, the emergent cultures—"seemed not to miss his freedom." In this interpretation of history we are not describing twentieth-century "realized worldliness" as the end of the road. Realized worldliness is not the permanent interpretation of life to which Christianity must become eagerly and pathetically relevant. It is not the kingdom which God in his freedom and grace alone can bring. It is not free in the sense that the Christian speaks of freedom in Jesus Christ. But the mechanisms of the world's response to the secularity of the times suggest by contrast which elements in Christian faith and life are not of interest to the world; further, one likes to think, the world's response parallels the kinds of possibility that exist in a vital world if a judging and redeeming

Christian word is spoken and lived. In this context those who invite Christianity to represent the last islands of security and shelter from a revolutionary world do it the disservice.

The parable in this setting is loaded with an exploitation of its intent. The reader need not agree with its relative judgment in detail; his observations of vitalities in church and world may differ. But concerning the mechanisms and substance of the world of secularity we can be more frontal. In the face of assertions concerning them several other alternatives are open.

One may disprove the documentation. He can retrace the secularizing centuries and say that we are misreading history. He must then prove how men's actions in the larger culture need God (the God of the Christian revelation, particularly) to locate the vast vacant interstellar spaces. How is God necessary, substantially, in political decision? Show us in Parliament, in Congress, in the Supreme Court. Who will point and document the "lo here!" or "lo there!" of God's finger in modern political history without being effectively countered by Christian and non-Christian alike? Is this interpretation of philosophy, education, art, faulty in that the norms and contents of Christian faith dominate in the whole culture? When the workaday scientist, craftsman, laborer, explorer, goes about his work, is the Bible his code, guide, and text? Does the Christian believe his enterprise would be significantly improved were it to become his code?

If this book's documentation (in broadest outline; we are not here quibbling over details of orthodox Copernicus, Pestalozzi, Jefferson, Darwin, Marx, Nietzsche, or Freud) is reasonably accurate, what is to be done? Can the world be put back into its earlier mold? Will it reject a new vitality for what it regards as an old bondage? How should Christians act? Shall they negate? Is Christ's Lordship limited to the millennium of Christendom?

Many Christians would reply that the best thing to do is to develop a para-culture, a pseudo-culture alongside the dominant culture of secularity. A parallel set of Christian institutions must be established. Set up schools, hospitals, laboratories, curricula, political parties, in which decidedly Christian norms can prevail. Eventually they may build up strengths to counter the larger culture effectively. The trouble with this tack is that this is not how the dynamics of culture have been working. The people who man the schools and laboratories often bring with them sets of assumptions that undercut this protective intention. Others would counsel a compartmentalized view of life. Be pious in your inner life; keep a sacred space around your faith. Let anything you want happen in your world of thought and action. Be at home in the world's city all week, and then paddle out to the sacred islands Sunday morning for a different view of the spiritual universe. This suggestion, too, breaks down. It is unfair to the Biblical counsel to participate concretely in life; it abandons the world to its own devices. More common than either of these approaches is a third, on which much Christian propagandizing is based today. The counsel: You never had it so good. Business as usual. In the middle of a secular world, filled as it is with religiousness and unreligiousness alike, men still join churches and build buildings. They will probably continue to do so. Do not ask basic questions of the content of their faith and its cultural effect or noneffect. Engage yourself in the institutional enterprise. Save souls. Drive the shiny new sedan to rescue people from the world of shiny new sedans. Raise funds from people to build buildings more impressive than their homes, so that the tall towers of Christianity can shadow new communities. Let the world go its way.

Karl Heim has compared this short-range strategy, which has an enormous popular appeal, to a sinking ship. For a time it is possible to keep the show going. On the deck the lights are lit, parties continue, people dance, the play goes on. The captain is on the bridge and the helmsman steers. Under the water line there is a great gaping hole and, despite all the pumping, the ship will certainly sink. Christians used the nineteenth century very creatively for the above-deck activities. They can hardly postpone for another century the task of involving all their members in the task of relating themselves to the "gaping hole" that a different understanding of life has occasioned. They are called again to love God with the mind as they often have shown they do with heart and soul. This task of relating will demand patient listening in the churches. It will engage not only theologians and academics; lovers and laborers, parents and horticulturists, businessmen and mourners, monks and mannequins, diners and pray-ers, will be called to find ways to bring together their current split-level existences.

One can forgive those who do nothing about the gaping hole because they never knew of it. In Christian thought—unlike Greek tragedy—ignorance is not so much a moral fault as it is a mark of the human condition. At the same time one must be critical of those who work to keep up appearances, to bluff the world, to make a show of bravado. Those who want to face the world may use other tactics. If they agree with this book and are discontented with "keeping up appearances," they may find other options.

Some, in panic, will react erratically and enter into self-preservative but false fanaticisms and alliances. Some will damn the world and abandon it. More will seek ententes with all who call themselves religious. Religion will become a buffer zone to nurture illusions over against secularity—a strategy in which the practical parallel between religiousness and nonreligiousness in our world is seldom perceived. Still others would, in the name of the Christian faith, make a new religion out of secularity and work to kill off all traces and residues, all lingering moments and monuments of Christian culture. The option this book presents is between these extremes. It is necessary to let everything be what it is. Where there is validity and vitality in the remnants of placed Christianity, they may continue their life even if they are not looked to with much hope for the future. One can learn from almost every enduring cultural event and artifact in the age of Christendom. Not all the lessons will be negative, by any means. Instead of killing off the deposits or worshiping a non-Christian culture, Christians can seek new relations to emerging cultures. Freed of anxiety over Christendom's occupied ground, they can work toward these relations without constant worry about the program or pattern for the future, without calculation at every turn. Christians begin: "We do not know what to do, but our eyes are upon thee' (II Chron. 20:12). And then, they do, they act.

Summary: <u>Faith precedes culture, it does not follow. Culture is the fruit of faith, not the foundation of it.</u> Christians in the past related themselves, often creatively, to the cultural possibilities of their day. We can learn from them.

4 THE HISTORY OF THE CHRISTIAN PLACE AND DISPLACEMENT

IF CHRISTIANS today live in a world of displacement, if the axioms of placed Christianity are threatened, the threats themselves may bear new possibilities for Christians who take responsibility for culture. Such Christians begin to see these possibilities by learning of past solutions. If so, it is time to see some of the ways in which men of faith in the past looked at the realities of Christian place and displacement.

In order to spare the general reader a technical treatise on life in the twelfth century (which we are not equipped to do) or in the nineteenth century (as we hope someday to do), this book will not consistently accent Christian memory. But certain milestones are important along the path; certain pegs are necessary on which to hang our understandings. There are precedents that suggest false turns and others that open paths. From some experiences we gain guidance and courage; from others we want to be rescued. The mythology of once-upon-a-time golden ages needs to be exploded so that we can be free to deal with the present. Certain slanders about the past need correction.

The pursuit of the past of such learning is handicapped by the fact that many people do not accustom themselves to listen to

historical witness. Some say, "History repeats itself," and look for
a model to past events which might be simply repeated. Others will
counter, "History is bunk," even though they are themselves
historians every time they recall an athlete's batting average, bet
knowingly on a horse race, or avoid a road which they remember
had potholes in it. But the wariness concerning historical evidence
can serve the argument of this book in at least this respect: the past
is not simply reproducible. We are not the early Christians, even
though we may learn a thing or two from them. We are but our
fathers' shadows cast at noon, says the student of Christian saint-
hood; but we have new shadows to cast. What are some of the
signs from the past?

The prototype for later Christian development is God's ancient
people of the old covenant. The Old Testament as appropriated in
the New, in particular, points to modes of seeing the cultural possibilities of faith in the life of wanderers. Abraham has already been
cited. His story begins with the promise of a land which remains
a promise to him. He moved with a real sense of the temporal: as
rich man, king, herdsman, actor, uncle, wanderer, doubter, man
of faith. He was at home in many places because he did not worship a place. In the Old Testament we hardly notice what Hebrews
11 points out: that he did not own the promised land. No legal tie
undergirded the institution and preservation of Abrahamic culture.
Intensity of faith, practical experience, vitality of expression, had
to serve.

The mobile, displaced life of Abraham is not seen as deplorable.
It was a situation in which the birth of real faith was particularly
to be noted. Deuteronomy 26:5 advises the worshiper when he
comes into the new land to say, "A wandering Aramean was my
father; and he went down into Egypt and sojourned there. . . ."
The Old Testament drenches us in a worldlinesses from which
Christians can still learn. It reveals countless kinds of bonds with
changing environments in wilderness and promised land. But the
characteristic tests of faith were in the characteristic situations of
exodus and exile.

Territorialism has its place; but territorialism and national zeal
also lead most readily to Israel's idolization of place and of a

specific culture. The prophetic voice was raised again and again to interrupt this worship of a specifically placed nation and culture. It is most clear in Amos 9:7:

> "Are you not like the Ethiopians to me,
> O people of Israel?" says the Lord.
> "Did I not bring up Israel from the land
>   of Egypt,
> and the Philistines from Caphtor and the Syrians
>   from Kir?"

The wilderness tabernacle suggested the kind of portability later associated with the discipleship of the New Testament. The preoccupation with details of adornment and governmental life on numberless pages of the Old Testament stands as a constant judgment on that Christian strand which claims to listen to the whole Bible yet speaks in anticultural terms of an interest only in snatching souls out of the world.

Not that the Old Testament does not envision hazards in nomadism and in exposure to many cultures. There are constant warnings against intermarriage, against adopting nice little cultural ceremonies from the environment—such as worshiping the Baalim, the convenient cult deities. The diagram of sacred space was apparent in the courts of the temple, the holy places. Coercion is implied in the setting aside of the Sabbath and the discipline of children.

What is more striking, however, is the kind of faith in Yahweh which asserts "Immanuel—God with us" in the concreteness of human experience. The relative indifference to details of the geography and furniture of the afterlife seems to have been the result of a kind of faith in the trustworthiness of a living God whose purposes are not exhausted by the places and times of the moment. When salvation is spoken of in the Old Testament, the root term often suggested is *yasha'*, which carries memories related to the idea of giving space, offering spaciousness, removing constriction, rescuing from the narrow passage. The Lord saved by bringing his children to a large place. The large place offered more possibility and—in the warfare of that day—more security. It was not a meaningless place, but a place where Yahweh guided as he once had guided with pillar and cloud. The large place killed the temptation to find security in idolizing the niches and nooks of the Baalim.

The Old Testament pictures are recalled in the New Testament and thus—in the eyes of Christians—acquire new importance. In the earliest New Testament writings, the Pauline letters, Abraham is again taken over as the example of the believer in the promise, one who was given few cultural props in face of the hope that he was to become the father of many nations. Paul's own missionary activity suggested the openness with which he rejected cultural supports in Palestinian memory and moved as a Roman (and thus world) citizen with his gospel. His activity must be seen in constant relief against the background of the leaders in Jerusalem. They conceived of the church as a cultural unit whose extensions must be examined, approved, checked at Jerusalem. They regarded—if we follow the narratives of the Acts of the Apostles— each new Christian community with suspicion. How could God work away from their sacred places? For Paul each receiving center became a sending center: Antioch, Corinth, Ephesus. Paul had a "desire to be with Christ, for that is far better." But "to remain in the flesh is more necessary on your account," and he moved across the terrain and the seascapes of his time with a cosmopolitan freedom that came from his knowing that his real commonwealth was in heaven. (See Phil. 1:19-26; 3:20.)

The movement of the Synoptics is doubly impressive. While we have refused to see the long compromise with history (in Ernst Troeltsch's observation)[1] which developed after the sense of the urgency and end-time were dissipated as a denial of the original vision—and therefore have refused to criticize the idea of a Christian culture—it is also important to see the original vision. In that there is hardly a hint of interest in a specific cultural cushion to support the call in a Christian place under the sun; rather, there is a positive refusal to form a counter-kingdom to occupy ground.

In the peculiar economy of Jesus' own ministry, restricted to the Jews for the most part, there is an apparent adherence to a specific place. (The motives for this restriction are too complex to be entered into here. None of the explanations that have been given is completely satisfying. In any case, the motives do not complicate our narrative.) Within the place in which he worked Jesus moved with his eye on his Father's eternal house and with a real at-homeness in the world. This gave him a sense of mobility. He may at times warn—or was it a complaint?—that foxes have holes and birds have nests, but he has no place, no home. The dialogical character of discipleship is clear: those who followed were also to share the displaced situation: "Follow me."

If we pursue the question of the groups of people who were identified with Jesus we see a wholly dynamic and mobile, displacing pattern. First was the attachment to the person of the Lord. Where Jesus was, there was the unit. Others rose to follow. He rejected their crowns and his enemy's temptation that he grovel for one. He needed no occupied ground, no specifically Christian culture, laws, arts, ethos, habits.

The second unit was discipleship. No "lo here!" or "lo there!" but "in your midst"—where he was, was the unit. The parables of the kingdom speak of actions, movement. Seeds grow secretly into great trees. Leaven works. Men plant. Seeds grow. Fishermen enlarge their catch. People go into fields. Following him was not a guarantee of place in the kingdom: it was a promise of a relation to God in many places. Some of the later Synoptic passages (particularly in Matthew) reveal the development of more static congregational life in the young *ekklesia*—(see Matt. 18), but for the most part the Synoptics involve the disciples in mobility, in "traveling light."

In the Acts and in Paul, again, the unit and the circle grow but remain portable. After Lordship and discipleship, the next step is the apostolate. People are sent out to baptize (baptism takes the place of the ethical conceptions of discipleship in the Synoptic Gospels); Christians are put out of the synagogue; those who received missionaries are to send on new ones. A fourth step is the development of colonies, *paroikiai,* "parishes" or gatherings of sojourners in Rome, Antioch, Corinth. The last glimpses are those in I Peter of Christians as aliens and exiles in a bewildered and hostile world.

In a careful exegetical study Paul Minear has isolated nearly one hundred *Images of the Church in the New Testament*. In the terms of this book, the vast majority of them are images of displacing, uprooting, nonconnection with a static or specific culture. There may be an occasional "sheltering" image such as the ark, but most are exposed: the people of God, the salt, the light, the leaven. Pentecost must certainly be seen as a displacing event: no longer only in one place is the name spoken to pilgrims. "We hear . . . in our own tongues the mighty works of God" (Acts 2:11).

The New Testament does not clearly decide what attitudes Christians should take toward existing cultures; there is great tension between the views of their possibility and their threat. In Romans 13 the religio-secular Roman government is described as instituted by God, as his agency, as God's servant for the Christian good. In Revelation 13 the same government (no doubt) is condemned in a revolutionary and destructive parable. What was determinative was not the detail of the culture but the more basic question of the believing response to God's call in the middle of any culture. There was little interest in the self-preservation, endowment, or prestige of the young Christian community.

The sacred Scriptures which determine so much of the impulse of Christian life do not commit Christians to one pattern of participation in cultural life. They do, however, more often envisage life in a displacing, dialogic setting. The church which listens to this revelation wisely remains open to both kinds of historical and social possibilities. Sociological adjustments should be as varied as theological position can anticipate.

If we move from the Biblical generations to the early Christian centuries, we see little decisive change. A tension does begin to develop between the missionary church, which is preoccupied with mobility and remains displaced, and the ordered church, preoccupied with the question of longer-range adaptation to the environment. Church order demanded a somewhat more diagrammatic and settled life. Which was more necessary? Do mobility and order exclude each other? Is there conflict between Matthew 18 and Matthew 28: "discipline the church" and "go out and make disciples of the whole world"? Here we need only observe that both tendencies were present.

In what ways does order take on the spatial model? It clears a space between church and world. It calls for self-exclusion from other cults (II Cor. 6:14-7:1; I Cor. 10:1-22). It makes room for the holy man and the ascetic who nurture the whole community by their intercessory and vicarious life. It develops officers in a routine life after the original charisms disappear. It augments its passion for doctrinal orthodoxy (the Pastoral Epistles). It grows more static in its interest in the bishop. Where the bishop is, there is the church; no Lord's Supper occurs without the bishop. It develops a canon of Scripture and a creedal tradition which stake out the limits of the corral in which the Christians may graze. It provides some elements of self-seeking institutionalism and new forms of rejecting responsibility for the Greco-Roman world.

One external agency, in these early Christian times, led to the further diagramming of life and placing of Christianity inside a specific culture. This was the opposition of a larger society which was not merely neutral. Persecution led Christians to their new place: the catacombs. What led to the persecutions is not the important question here; failures on the part of both church and culture to communicate intention played a large role. But some Christians stayed above ground, too. Justin Martyr was as eager to relate to Jewish thought and Greek philosophy (in a sort of cultural liberalism) as he was willing to remain faithful if that cultural environ called him to martyrdom. Tertullian could insist that Christians were the most loyal of the Romans and on the other hand could ask the cultural question: What part does Athens have with Jerusalem? At the height of the persecutions the Christians were largely displaced, not at home with many elements of culture.

In the perspective of this historical survey, one of the two most dramatic changes in the socio-cultural setting of the church in all history came about early in the fourth century.

Christianity, for the first time, had its place. It was a counter-kingdom. It occupied ground. It had space under the sun. Ordinarily the hinge on which this change can be hung—the cluster of documents now referred to as the Edict of Milan—is dated in the time of Constantine and his successors around A.D. 313. While the change was basically legal in character, it affected all the church's relations to culture. Aspects of the picturesque, passionate, and sometimes unhappy episode that Santayana labeled romantic Christendom were coming to birth. The Roman Empire (later, in both its Western and Eastern phases) officially adopted the Christian faith. Soon Christianity was using the sword to consolidate its place; except for an occasional relapse or two, it soon arrived at the point where it could use the sword to enforce its claim and persecute others.

Someday the conventional periodization of church history into early, medieval, reformation, and modern may be revised to do justice to this dramatic change. If "early" means pre-Christendom and "modern" means post-Christendom, Medieval-Reformation are really two phases of one era, Christendom. We have already dissented from Santayana's reference to Christendom's unhappy character. Few historical eras can be written off so conveniently with adjectives. The Protestant view of the fifth to ninth centuries as Dark Ages is justified. There was a real darkness. But the putting out of the lights was not all that happened in the Catholic phase of Christendom in the barbarian age. In recent decades, scholars in the whole church have come to regard more positively the Catholic responsibility for a millennium of Western European culture. Gothic cathedrals, books of hours, Aquinian theology, the rise of universities, monastic culture—these and other traces of Middle-Age culture—have been explored and gratefully recovered.

A sweeping assertion sums up the phase called Christendom: Christianity had a place. Fortunately, it was a large place: Eastern and Western empires; northern barbarian and southern civilian in the Western empire; Pope and Emperor; cleric and lay—there were many cultural elements which kept the faith from being stifled by the weight of a monolith. The theoretician in the hinge period, St. Augustine, in his *City of God* provided a Catholic charter for the rich life of the following millennium. In the mode of his day and drawing on one-half of the Biblical witness to the nature of the world, Augustine was largely negative in his orientation to the world. Yet he cannot be understood apart from his real love for *Romanitas* and Rome, and those who would write a new *City of God* for the age after Christendom must work with his vision of the two cities as the basic document. After Augustine, the high point comes in the ninth century, in the Carolingian period. In the court of Charlemagne a political, cultural, social reality was fused for a moment. The idea of a Christian culture was all but incarnate. The Carolingian resolution was not a dull, monolithic pattern; creative tensions remained within it. But in that era some idea of how a Christian culture could look came into view. The church had a place. The world no longer had to be fought around the church; it had to be fought, rather, within the church (hence, monastic reforms on repeated occasions).

The Christian culture of high Christendom had as its strength the fact that it was believed in. It was not a skeleton calling for explanation, a museum of curiosities calling for curators. In our picture purloined from Kafka, the church was the panther, old Rome and newer barbarians—the hunger artists with no taste for the food of life—had spent themselves. To say that this Christian culture was believed in does not mean that faith came easier to its contemporaries. It merely points to the fact that the theoretical treatises, the royal and papal actions, the arts and artifacts, and the practical actions of enough people in common life and in decisive situations affirmed the positive side of this culture.

An aside: Just as the Reformation became necessary to rescue Christianity after Christendom was no longer believed in in the same way, so today a reformation becomes necessary to rescue Christianity from Protestantdom in those parts of the world where that episode has become but a romantic memory, no longer generative or vital.

During the high medieval period, in the first of Christendom's two climaxes, the double-sided character of Christian institutions became apparent. Thus the papacy was on occasion the protector of the culture and at other times the patron of missions (as with Augustine in England, and others who worked at papal behest). Monasticism, the corollary and the check to papacy, was on occasion the protector of the culture in the cloister and at other times it was the base for missions (the *peregrini,* the wandering saints of the middle ages). The sects, an irritant to both papacy and monastics, rose to protect Christians from the world and provide for themselves a new place; on the other hand, some of them engaged in missionary activities.

Out of the creative tensions within and between these movements came the climax of the medieval. The systems, syntheses, cathedrals, universities, may not have been so neat and comprehensive as the romantics who raise St. Thomas Aquinas and the Gothic to normative status would have it. But at least we get glimpses and tenuous holds. An empire (in both its parts) was called Christian; the church dominated in it and often over it. The barbarian was converted and the infidel (often) defeated in crusades. Syntheses were actually worked at and worked out. But the phase was a phase, the moment passed. Even at the moment of the climax, signs of disintegration were setting in. In the act of religionizing the culture, men had also succeeded in secularizing the church. This gave rise to calls for reforms that became disruptive.

The church in many ways gave aid to the rising local loyalties of national states, loyalties which were to turn against it. The church in the universities had to encourage the new sciences, philosophy, and linguistic studies which led to the humanistic ancestors of secularity. Christendom in its Catholic phase was durable but not normative. Protestants and Catholics alike borrow, often unthinkingly, many of its modes of life and mission. But the heart went out of it early. Its place was challenged by empire and nation. Its synthesis began to be neglected and then criticized. The universities were not docile nurseries of the faith. Scholastic philosophy itself produced a heresy called nominalism; this in turn was an instrument in the hands of some of the pre-Reformers.

Here, as so often (as with Constantine, or Thomas Jefferson), the decisive turn came on political grounds. Joachim of Fiore envisioned an apocalyptic kingdom that would have no patience with a Christian culture. Marsilius of Padua developed explicitly anti-Petrine, anti-papal political theories. Some of the documents on which Christian territorial claims were based were proved forgeries by devotees of the growing science of historical criticism.

What followed—what we have come to call the sixteenth-century

Protestant Reformation—was not from this viewpoint a revolution or an adjustment. (That statement is not intended to minimize the radical theological differences but to point to a cultural continuity.) The year 1517, when Luther proposed the Ninety-five Theses, was not in this context the turn to modernity so much as was Thomas Jefferson and James Madison's reversal of Constantine in Virginia in 1774. The division between Eastern and Western churches in 1054 represented a change to two "places" in which Christianity was at home; in 1517 a multiplication of places began.

The Reformation settlement, so far as the reality of placed Christianity is concerned, was partial. In general, territorialism was the principle in church life, and the map of Europe to this day reflects the settlements. Calvin's Genevan theocracy was characteristic. The saints would rule; the state's laws and its education, its entertainment and its moral pattern, must pass the scrutiny of the Christian elite. Anglicanism settled for an England that could waver from Protestant to Catholic phase again and again, but pluralism in the modern sense was not anticipated. Scotland was to be a Presbyterian monolith. Luther's theories on two realms were not really effected in the territorial settlement in Germany. The princes and nobles signed most of the Reformation documents in that country. Some of the sects, it is true, practiced withdrawal from the world; more practiced withdrawal from established churches and themselves set up—or tried to—theocracies and "places" of their own.

It remains as dust under the Protestant rug that in no large area, in no major settlement, did the Reformation completely triumph without the help of the civil power and sometimes the sword. The New World was not yet born. In 1555 at the Peace of Augsburg the principle became formal. *Cuius regio, eius religio* was a static geographical settlement if there ever was one: whoever was prince of the region was determiner of the religion of the region. Reformation thought for the most part was uninterested in missions because of its preoccupation with Christendom's settled sense of place. Holy wars were fought for the Christian places. *Landeskirchen*, territorial churches, established churches, became customary, to remain incarnate and go stale in the kinds of Christendom Søren Kierkegaard had to attack in the nineteenth century.

The partly self-contradictory Reformation settlement accounts for some ambiguous attitudes in modern national life. Often those churches which most accent separation of church and state are most insistent on seeing formal, legal interaction of the two in national affairs. Such a voice belongs to a transitional generation in Protestantism; the realized pluralism in America is throwing evangelical Christianity back on a set of resources different from those with which it first worked on the American scene. The settlements of 1555 did not anticipate the next revolution, the growth of secularity. When the next self-contained pattern of worldliness emerged it was seldom seen to have possibilities for the church.

After the decisive era of the Protestant episode came the second hinge-point in church-society relations on the legal level. Its effects are still being felt, and some of the changes it is destined to bring about are only now being worked out in many nations. While this kind of displaced situation is itself a stepson of the Reformation, sons of the Reformation are still busy trying to understand it. In 1774, in Virginia, there began that process in American life wherein Congress was prohibited from making laws respecting establishment of religion (even though nine of the thirteen colonies had establishments). The states followed suit; the last tall towers tumbled in Connecticut and Massachusetts by 1833-34. Since that date church and state have been separate in the formal legal sense. But in the mores, in the subtler coercions of social pressure, the churches have been established right down into our own time. Many actions of the church are dependent upon a Christian interpretation of American history that does not do justice to history or to the actual legal stance of America. In our own time many Protestants are restive over the question whether they should participate in killing off the last residues of their empire or merely let them die.

The American settlement was complex in its origins. In part it was practical: competing establishments would not countenance one central establishment. In part it was the product of modernity's disruption of the diagrammatic: people moved from colony to colony and in their mobility resented paying for religions they did not believe in. In part it was the product of new emphases in old establishments: most of the Virginia secularizers of the state were nominal and sometimes practicing Anglicans. James Madison's form of Presbyterianism had a profound effect. Even more: new religious emphases, which had been muffled in Europe, were coming into their own in America. Baptist, Quaker, and other "sectarian" voices were heard on the side of the practical solutions. As a parallel—or an undercutter—of them all was that peculiar American brand of Enlightenment thought that, in the name of nature's God and the self-evidence of things, abhorred particular religious emphases. Since this emphasis provided the most articulate undertone of ideology behind the settlement, most American Christians, Protestant and Roman Catholic alike, are reduced to sounding rationalist in their religion whenever they appeal for a religious or Christian America on the basis of the founding documents.

In the modern world many establishments remain. In England the one hundredth Archbishop of Canterbury speaks in favor of disestablishment. Spain's establishment relies for its hold on coercive if not totalitarian power, and any revolutionary change would certainly jostle this place. The Scandinavian establishments are not vital and the other continental forms of legal support for religion are of waning importance. The direction is unmistakably away from *cuius regio, eius religio,* away from Augsburg, Canterbury, and Geneva, and toward the ideas of Jefferson, Madison, and final disestablishment.

5 THE NEW WORLD:

FIRST AND SECOND

CHANCES IN CULTURE

THE NEW WORLD represents the new thing in church life: the opportunity to study the background of pluralism and secularity along with an energetic voluntary response in Christian institutions. In its most far-reaching stages the displacement of Christendom is being seen in one of the nations which has produced as large a percentage of active churchgoers as any major nation of our time. What is the stance of America today, in the age after Protestantdom?

America has long known that its new experiment in church life would subject it to the scrutiny of the Christian world. Christians in other nations concurred with a minority in the new United States that Jefferson would succeed in doing what he—arch infidel that he was—wanted to do: throw the churches on their own resources and thus kill them. Others saw in the new world a prototype and pattern which Christians everywhere, were they wise, would follow. Lessons learned in the United States could be of help to Christians operating in Europe's "post-Christian" climate and in the missionary fields that never became formally Christian.

By some of its religious settlers, America was regarded as a

55

wilderness. This recalls the early church's attitude toward the Roman Empire: it was unknown, virgin territory with many tangled kinds of possibilities. Others came to America, seeing it as Zion, a fortress or stronghold. This vision recalls the bastion view of medieval Europe; such settlers wanted to establish for themselves a legally protected Christian place. What came to pass was a frustration of both intentions.

In the eyes of many, America began as a great religious and even Protestant nation and has, through the years, experienced a diminishing of this character. It would be much more accurate to say that the colonial period in America saw a strong Protestant elite, a populace with Protestant memories, an even more decisive "Enlightenment" elite of statesmen. Then, in the early national period, in the nineteenth century, it became a Protestant empire;[1] it occupied ground and had a settled place.

For Protestants, America was a promised land. In New England and Virginia they were permitted to set up their own legal versions of religion. In the middle colonies, as in Pennsylvania, they were extended freedom of religion and freedom from religion if they wanted it. In this promised land Protestants grew to statistical majority. If in the colonial period our scientific guesses turn up a population that was "church-affiliated" by present standards to a degree of only 5 or 10 per cent, that situation changed gradually until in our own time about 64 per cent of the people can be found on church rolls. The legislative record of the earliest colonies and of the nineteenth century and the early twentieth reveals the presence of Protestantism as a power bloc and as a suasive force. The history of America's mores and rhetoric cannot be written without careful understanding of this phenomenon.

If Protestantism formed a foundation in the New World, the Catholic house developed there peculiarly in the nineteenth century. Immigration, natural population increase, and then discipline and mission accounted for a Catholic growth which has outstripped Protestant growth for many decades. Judaism was represented by a tiny minority in colonial times and has now come to be a decisive minority in the urban power centers. Other religions were accepted, if sometimes with suspicion, and there was always plenty of room for quiet nonreligion or apathy in the face of the churches' claims.

In this twentieth century America has tended to become the religious nation it was by its early baptisms—paradoxically, at the moment when historic Christian nations were turning their backs on religion. Quite as paradoxically, the growth of the religious communities served chiefly to heighten America's latent pluralism, and a new understanding of national life has come about in the age of displacement and intersectionality. Pluralism was latent from the time when, in early seventeenth-century days, two men of different religious persuasions set foot on the shores of English-speaking America. But its openness became the daily experience of Americans only when space for separation was gone; when population growth, mobility, transportation and communication, urbanism, and other factors served to displace the islands, jostle people, and crisscross their value systems.

Pluralism is displacing Protestantdom in America, much to the discomfort of those who misread American history as the building of an empire or a place where Protestants would have the cards stacked in their favor. The new situation is here to stay. It will be revealed as more and more dominant, and any church pattern which does not relate to it is living on borrowed time. The styles of thought of Americans are changing; the courts are recognizing the change. The voices of organized religion and the strident voices of the insecure will often be raised in tones to criticize the secularism of national life, but few will be ready to pay the price for a reversal of the trend. All the documentable social forces, most of the trends in interpreting life, run counter to the Protestant empire idea.

In the new situation churches can plead pluralistic ignorance; they can shut their eyes to change. Or they can be stunned into immobility, numbed by the recognition of change. They can capitulate unthinkingly to erosive forces in national life. Or they can seek ways to criticize and then positively to relate to a newly realized unfolding. Dedicated Christian thinkers may find themselves in surprising alliance with many outside the church to bring about such a relation.

To some, the counsel that the churches relate themselves positively to the new situation looks like a retreat. Rituals invoking the names of the Founding Fathers are regularly recited. But it must be asked substantively what detail in the religion of the Founding Fathers specifically relates to distinctive Christian witness. That there is much misunderstanding on this point within the Protestant community near the end of the second third of the twentieth century is clear. To those who insist on a Christian kingdom in America the newer Protestant advocates of positive relations to pluralism appear to be prophets of gloom, masochists, rejoicing in misfortune. To them any talk of "post-Protestant" cultural emphases looks like an attention-getting device to instill panic and promote the sale of books.

The Protestant who advocates new kinds of relations to the world and to pluralist culture is coming to prevail, however, and ought to be understood. Most of the students of American religious life in the departments of history, sociology, and usually theology in the major seminaries (Winthrop Hudson, Franklin Littell, Edwin Scott Gaustad, are names that come to mind instantly among historians; Peter Berger symbolizes the antiestablishment sociologists) are associated with the second-glance view. While there is realism in their historical analysis, there is also ordinarily a patient interest in the development of new Christian forms, an interest that can hardly be characterized as cynicism or despair.

American Protestantism has not until now had to experience a reformation. It is used to revivals and declines, but reformation in its self-understanding has not occurred. Protestant is what the unreflective American has been; Protestantism is the religion that "comes naturally," just like the proverbial "talking in prose." Protestant is what one is if he does not take pains to disassociate himself from the established background. Such a religious attitude can hardly generate exciting interpretations of life or authentic ethical impulses. The basic fact of American life and religious life today is its pluralism—a displacing fact as far as any Christian empires are concerned. Coping with this reality has become the first item on many agenda.

Three attitudes, in my observation, characterize Protestantism's view of pluralism and of the secularity that is its corollary in America today. All of them are reflective of the change from the day when Protestantism's place was unchallenged. In 1927 André Siegfried could call Protestanism America's only national religion; to misunderstand this would be to misunderstand national life. In 1936 H. Richard Niebuhr[2] could still quote this statement with favor. In 1962 the Jesuit magazine could more aptly characterize the new *America*: it was dominated by a "strong residual Protestant cultural tradition." "Residual" refers to the assumption that there was more here last year than there is now and that there will be less next year than now. It places Protestant culture in a recessional. Once there were trumpets; now there is only the muffled drum of the rear guard. Once there was volume; now there is a long diminuendo. Americans who disagreed with *America* in other respects did not disagree with its summary of religious life: the phrase expressed an intuitive and broadly accepted view. What to do with the memory and the residuum?

Within Protestantism, three options are live. One stresses the idea of "business as usual." Do not notice the problem and it will go away or it can be postponed. Call this "Protestantism without pluralism." A second option would work to counteract the situation; aggressively it would seek to win back the ground it occupied, the place it held. This can be termed "Protestantism against pluralism." The third, "Protestantism in pluralism," seeks redefinitions and a new course of action in the setting in which Protestantism will inevitably live. Say that Protestantism today is the wallpaper in the furnished mental apartment that Americans live in. The first or oblivious group would not notice that the paper is fading. The second would retouch and revivify the paper. The third would tend to say: Don't worry about the wallpaper; if the guest notices it, that is all right. But let us concern ourselves with furnishing the apartment. Provide the sofas and paintings, lamps and carpets, the instruments of function and beauty.

Those who wish to remain oblivious concerning the pluralist environment do the lesser disservice to Protestantism. They are easily dismissible by the larger community and do not necessarily complicate the whole evangelical mission. They might write the "church-tower history" of the generation and suggest to the people in their environs that they do not really know what is going on. But in a sense their position is harmless.

The counterattacking position which seeks to keep up appearances, to hold on to previously occupied ground, represents a more difficult problem. The insecurities induced by change often produce erratic action. One instance should illumine the problem. It is not casually chosen; rather it relates to the most significant symbolism of the recent past: the event which summarized the change from Protestant to pluralist America in the public consciousness; namely, the Presidential campaign of 1960.

John Kenneth Galbraith in *The Liberal Hour*[3] has pointed out how few events really reach to the roots of public consciousness. Only one or two events in a generation or even a century are profound enough to cause changes in national patterns of voting on a permanent basis. Thus the two World Wars, far-reaching as their devastation was, remained foreign wars which did not touch the psyche of every American. The American Civil War, however, is still reflected in voting patterns, daily living, folk culture. So, too, is the economic depression of the 1930s. It reached into homes of rich and poor alike. It staggered the aged, shaped the attitudes of the maturing, determined the childhood of the generation now coming into power. The permanent complex of anxiety and complacency caused by the Cold War is perhaps a third case in point.

In American religious life the same general principle probably holds true. Only two or three events on the American continent have had sufficient symbolic weight to change basic ways of looking at life. The far-reaching effects of voluntaryism, separating church and state, is one of the axioms of American religious life because of the events of the first half century of nationhood. The religious "winning of the West" with its evangelical fervor, its revivalism, also determines many current ways of thinking about religion.

The Presidential campaign of 1960 was a third event in this category. Until then no American President had been "non-Protestant" in the sense of his not being able to blend into the background. The United States has had numbers of Unitarian or Universalist Presidents whose religious profession would not fit into conventional Protestant patterns of expression, but this fact was easily disregarded. The United States also had numbers of Presidents who were notably casual about their religious profession, but this too was easily forgotten. Only a Jewish or Roman Catholic President would change the picture. The President as he goes about his chores is often involved in rituals and liturgies of folk religion and a national faith. So long as he was non-Jewish or non-Catholic his mannerisms and expressions could give substance to the afterglow of Protestant and "Enlightenment" witness of early America. His church attendance could be reported on without arousing great interest; it would merely be "the thing to do."

Should a President be elected whose profession ran counter to the expected, a profound change would be effected. The American environment had been seen to be somehow redemptive and revelatory when faced with the Protestant witness. But Catholic thought and witness, to Catholic and non-Catholic alike, appears to proceed from an arcanum alien to this environment. Should a President be elected who as priest and liturgist of national religion drew on outside resources, the real—that is, pluralistic—character of national life would be newly revealed.

Certainly this subtle yet deep fear of change was at the root of the more effective anti-Catholicism of the 1960 election campaign. This is not the place to enter into all details of the matter. The immaturity of the American Catholic community was revealed in its treatment of the issue; nonreligious editors and columnists were blind to the fact that others besides Protestants can be bigots. Even the strident anti-Catholic groups can legitimately claim that they were often misunderstood. One may also concur with those who suggest that religion can properly be an issue in a Presidential campaign; that a candidate's Catholicism, Mormonism, Christian Scientism, or Presbyterianism must be reckoned with in a view of the whole man. One can even share some anxieties over exploitation of the religious issue (e.g., the Democratic party's overuse of Mr. Kennedy's televised encounter with the Houston Protestant clergy), the danger of future bloc voting, and the possibility of confusion in matters of church and state in the instance of Catholicism also.

These questions sometimes were raised in the campaign and often provided the respectable front for the subterranean issue that revealed itself again and again. That issue: the insecurity of the Protestant community or the non-Catholic, non-Jewish element that associates itself with Protestantism in the interpretation of national life. An instance of the inclusiveness of this concern was the most important religious event of the campaign, a gathering (somewhat unfairly termed the "Peale" group after Norman Vincent Peale) which met in Washington, D.C. during the campaign.

This meeting attracted Protestants ("and other Americans") of a number of political stripes, though the tendency was toward the conservative element. It also attracted people of opposite religious colors, from extremely liberal to extremely fundamentalist. It would be almost impossible to envision any other issue that could attract such a gathering. Their interpretations of Catholicism, tolerance, and national life would vary widely. But the press releases, the news conferences, the trickles of information, and the ongoing participation of many attendants revealed a consistent theme: fear lest the once-Protestant complex of the nation change, fear lest the now-pluralist character of the nation be revealed. The subsequent election of Mr. Kennedy effected just that: no profound political change came about, but the symbolism of President as quasi-Protestant priest was changed. The election did lead to the coming of age of much of the Protestant community. The inevitability of change, the new understanding of American power structures, became part of the Protestant consciousness. The event has made discussion of this theme plausible and possible.

Many of the people at the Washington meeting were men of goodwill, not Nativists or fossils from the Know-Nothing era. But their reading of national life does not provide a real option. Their rear-guard brethren serve only to continue to complicate the problem. Thus a congressional coterie, with some public support, regularly turns up with a Christian Amendment to the Constitution. It would announce to the world that America is based on the law of Jesus Christ and is serving him in the world. (That many Roman Catholics concur not only in such moves but in many Protestant attacks on the secularizing of national life reveals the extent of the rationalist-Protestant state of mind in the American lineage.)

The trauma and the readjustment of 1960 have ushered in a new day of interpretation for Protestants. For the first time serious interest in the choice of futures has been aroused and many publications have had opportunities to describe the choices. Shall Protestants ignore the wallpaper; or shall they be charged with the furnishing of the American psychic apartment? As the outlines and lineaments of the decisions begin to take shape it is well to pause and look at the issues involved. There are, it is to be admitted, disadvantages as well as advantages for Protestants if they choose to come to terms with the pluralist reality and do not work just to keep up appearances or to regain previously occupied ground.

The possible disadvantage: To participate in furnishing the room, to lose interest in being the wallpaper, may mean killing off some kinds of vitalities that were useful to nation and church. Protestantism's dialogue with its environment in the past produced some remarkably fruitful results: The religious outlook of the unorthodox yet evangelical American theologian Abraham Lincoln was informed by this dialogue. Much that was salutary in the American past grew out of picturesque, passionate, often happy romantic Protestantdom. What would Protestantism in pluralism, what would American secularity, produce? A venture is involved in the choice. Further, as the wallpaper, as the taken-for-granted aspect of the religious culture, Protestantism did provide a comfortable, welcoming, familiar, and homey background. Would it have the nation's ear if, like Catholicism and Judaism, it spoke from an arcane treasury, from a distance?

At the same time there are advantages in choosing to come to terms with pluralism. In the strange dynamics of religion in culture, a particular religion will customarily receive blame and criticism for what is wrong in the culture but will not receive credit for its positive contributions. This can burden its decisively religious witness. The obvious illustration is the medieval record. Today's Protestant typically knows all about the less admirable side of medieval life—the vices—the superstition, darkness, the mistreatment of peoples—and blames the Roman Catholic Church. But at the same time today's Protestant is also the inheritor of much that was excellent in the medieval culture. If he is conservative, he apes its architecture. He sends his children to universities whose structure points back to medieval patterns. He is heir to a civilization that might have yielded to the barbarian had not papacy and monasticism worked to create and vitalize the culture. He does not usually give credit to Roman Catholicism for these positives.

So with American national life. Anticolonial and fanatic new nationalist movements in Africa and Asia, in their rejection of America, will often turn on the Protestant missionary as the representative of an imperialist and exploitative culture. No one can read nineteenth-century missionary history and say that that is all the missionaries were. But they hitchhiked on the travels, stowed away on the vessels of those who represented an empire that is now being shrugged off. Today's American youth grows up with stereotypes of the unexciting and often bigoted background of Protestant nineteenth-century culture but is not often made aware of the virtues of the evangelical deposit in culture. A religious group which is near enough to the larger community to have a measure of its confidence and which is far enough away to have something novel to say is in a better position.

In any campus situation where representatives of various faiths and nonfaiths speak, greatest expectation is brought to those who represent the furniture of American life, not the wallpaper. The rabbi and the priest, the agnostic or the Zen Buddhist—these may have something to say as speakers who bring a perspective derived in part from the outside. The Protestant clergyman may be listened to for his cleverness and dexterity in reasserting the platitudes which hold the culture together. But so far as his having something important to say is concerned, expectations are low. This cozy and taken-for-granted relation to culture goes some distance to explain a general lack of imagination in the Protestant literary community. The Jewish novelist (of the Saul Bellow era) as the uprooted, alienated, displaced urbanite formed the parables of dislocation of the time. The Roman Catholic writer shares the same parables. But the Protestant writer is too much at home in a waning culture to speak with interest of an emerging world. Realization of Protestantism's position in pluralist and secular America will no doubt provide a new setting, and the complicated task of relating witnesses, meshing gears, finding home, should provide new parables.

Should the coming generation of Protestants vote that the advantages of the "Protestantism in pluralism" option outweigh the disadvantages, and should they so participate with freedom in a cultural environment where change has occurred, we may look for much that is new. There would then be less interest in the legal prerogatives, the coercive power of the churches. There would be less self-advertisement on their part, less concern over their good name; less anguish over their endowments and tax exemptions. There could be new freedom to minister to the larger community.

The current pictures of Protestantism, in the opinion of the critical young Protestant or the outsider, reveal the way in which, after Protestantdom's breakdown, the institutional self-interest serves to confuse evangelical witness. Sociologists have for some time been bringing these pictures to us. At last they are beginning to take effect. Peter Berger[4] has observed that the sociological uncertainty of the church provokes more anguished and creative discussion than any other current threat, including the changed way of looking at life associated with names such as Darwin, Freud, Nietzsche, Marx. Separate a Protestant layman from his religious premises and get him to speak about religious institutions, and his answers to questions will strikingly parallel those of the nonchurched.

The massive silhouette the churches (Catholic as well as Protestant) create on the American skyline is that of a self-preservative institutionalism. The clergyman exists as promoter of the organization. Most of its outlines and means of garnering loyalties are seen to parallel the mechanisms employed by labor unions, management organizations, service clubs. Since the institutional self-interest preoccupies the churches and does not directly serve the community, it seems to incarnate irrelevance and even "bad faith." The social and cultural signals they emit—as institutions, and they are universally seen to emit these signals—have an impact on the lives of their adherents, but they are usually predictably grooved in the safe presuppositions of the middle class, away from the dreams and frustrations of both the laboring elements and the elites of national life, to say nothing of the aspiring peoples around the world.

As one form of the national establishment, dependent so often on the goodwill of the generally religious larger community, the churches are usually seen to be domesticated, socially irrelevant in a revolutionary world. They are said to attract the least controversial and least exciting elements in the community. They are successful and will continue to be so, but their successes abstract and distract them from the type of service to the world to which they have been called.

By no means are these uniquely Protestant problems; it could well be argued that Catholicism as it moves into the American mainstream and displaces elements of Protestantism will inherit many of the problems. The enormous institutional enterprise of Catholicism—someone has to pay for coal bills, schools, and statues—has forced on it an economically self-preservative attitude that complicates its picture in national life. In the future it will no doubt be more vocal in its defense of its tax exemptions, privileges, endowments, than are Protestants. It may also have to pay the price: blending into the wallpaper.

Recently historians have begun to point to certain advantages accruing to religious groups that did not belong to the American "mainstream." A combination of factors has given the place for churches in this elusive mainstream. These forces are confusing. Statistics do not tell the whole story. Congregationalism, which belongs, has for decades been fairly small in the statistical picture. Nor will polity explain the situation. Historically, Episcopalianism had been seen as a "nondemocratic" body and yet was thoroughly welcomed in the democratic climate. Class structure played a part; the upper middle class formed the mainstream. Influential members helped; nose-counting in *Who's Who* helped keep some denominations there. Theological generalizations, on the other hand, did little to keep a given denomination in an advantageous position.

In general, the mainstream was originally made up of the white

Anglo-Saxon religious forces which issued into American life past Plymouth Rock or up Chesapeake Bay, via New England or Virginia. This first wave (Congregational-Presbyterian-Episcopalian) was joined by a second that came into its own somewhat later. The Baptist-Methodist-Disciples of Christ cluster arrived at accepted status in the double movement of the early nineteenth century: the struggles for religious liberty, in which most of them participated; and in the expansion and religious awakening of the frontier and the West in which they were more successful than the other denominational cluster.

In the middle of the twentieth century a new family of denominations in Protestantism is accepted, along with Catholicism, as part of the mainstream. In general, these denominations entered American life *via* the middle colonies, particularly Pennsylvania. Many of them were of Continental and thus of foreign-language-speaking provenance. For the most part, while loyally they did share in the defense and growth of the nation, they were immune to, and thus were less eroded by, many theological and ideological issues of the late nineteenth century. (Social Darwinism, Fundamentalism *vs.* Modernism, etc.). Among these groups were the German Reformed, which came into its own somewhat earlier than others. This denomination produced the Niebuhr brothers, who dominated American theology from the 1930s into the 1960s. It welcomed German theologians of the evangelical churches who were not always at ease in American Lutheranism. It has since merged with a typical earlier mainstream denomination, Congregationalism.

This "third wave" includes, along with the Reformed, the Lutheran, Mennonite, Brethren families and others of the left wing of the Continental Reformation. Whether or not they will bring something distinctive to the understanding of pluralism is, however, open to question. These newly emergent groups sometimes feel under pressure to prove their "at-homeness" in the wallpaper pattern, and to minimize their own heritage and peculiar assets. Theological self-criticism in the old-line denominations can prepare such older groups to play new distinctive roles.

What appears to be needed from all three of these waves is the

American environment's still generally positive attitude to the revelatory element in religion. Some excitement must be brought to the task as the Word of God is related to the world of men in a new world of experiment. With this must come a drawing on resources not wholly captive to this environment—resources in Biblical, patristic, medieval, Reformation thought as well as in today's secular world.

Too great an intimacy, too much familiarity with the general environment, has limited Protestants in their relation to the emerging awareness of pluralism. For pluralism has its own set of problems. Like secularity, it is not the unfolding of the kingdom of God. It is an assertion concerning how the cards of history are dealt, an awareness of things as they are. It can be instrument or trap; hence, it is best to deal with it consciously and matter-of-factly.

The danger in the new awareness of pluralism is that it may serve to sophisticate the generalized, unreformed, and unredeemed national religious consciousness. Americans have long been inclined to look for a consensus (some even seek an ideology) which would lubricate the processes of national life and glue its elements together. The post-World War II talk of pluralism has seemed to offer such a consensus. Should not the conversations between faiths produce a common faith, nationally utile? This hope is understandable but carries danger. When we speak of a common religion, it is not enough to speak only of attitudes; content and substance must be dealt with. Unless they are, unless religion has a definable substance apart from national life, what shall protect it against becoming a mere instrument of the state? One recalls the ideological religion which the *Deutsche Christen,* the German Christians, devised to celebrate the Third Reich's national consensus. It was impotent to extricate itself from National Socialist ideology.

Consensus-religion has other liabilities. A religion must have a generating center to motivate ethics, the fabrication of culture, theology. The Jew finds his center in the Torah; the Roman Catholic, in the grace mediated by the Church; and the Protestant, in Biblical revelation and the unfolding life of the church. The religious undefined experience of the nation, elusive and aiming to combine and not to offend the particular religions, has no such impulse center, no source. In the past Protestantism as such served to provide much of the consensus-religion. In the new setting distinctive Protestantism no longer can do this, and it is this displacement that makes caretakers of the Protestant museum uneasy.

Protestantism cannot serve as a kind of consensus-religion for a number of reasons. For one thing, the other religious elements, especially Catholicism, Judaism, and an ill-defined humanism, are now wholly exposed to public consciousness. None of them will be content with a continued assertion of Protestant verities as the national consensus. What has happened in the public schools is an illustration. For a century, secularism was stayed or staved off in the public schools by a semi-licit and ill-defined pattern of religious observances that had a general Protestant source and orientation. (When in local communities of Jewish dominance Jewish holidays and observances were noticed, when in Catholic communities that faith's accents were heard in the public school, there were ordinarily protests. The distinctiveness of generalized Protestant observance had gone unnoticed; Protestantism was "part of the wallpaper"). The new pluralist environment settles first for innocuous, insubstantial prayers (such as the twenty-two-word incantation written for public schools by the New York Board of Regents and rejected by the Supreme Court in 1962) and later for a nonreligious situation.

Again, Protestantism cannot serve well as the base for a consensus religion because it is, in general, uneasy over natural law and natural religion. These, in the past, were the strings with which Western Christians could latch their distinctiveness into the general experience. And were Protestantism to attempt to serve for the consensus in the new environment, it would soon see itself manipulated into an ideology. Its free-flowing past forms would not be sufficiently functional to fill the demands of those who seek an ideological weapon "to provide national purpose" or to "show up atheistic Communism."

Protestantism in the new setting can serve best by being faithful to its generating center. It listens in a way of its own to the divine revelation; then in a disciplined church life it is open to the pluralist conversation and to secularity as such. <u>Given the alternatives: Protestantism as a renewed national religion; Protestantism as the unrecognized undergirding of consensus-religion; non-Protestant consensus-religion; and secularity as the character of official national life—the last seems the most wise, creative, and workable solution.</u>

Critics of this view abound. They should clearly state alternatives. Their Protestant-based consensus-religion will have, must have, a substance. What is it? Is their definition fair to the genius of Protestantism? Will their outline be acceptable to Catholics, Jews, and others? If not, will it be faithful to the genius of national life? Will it be helpful to domestic and international policy? What are its sources and norms? Who will administer it? Who are the priests and functionaries? What safeguards does it possess against development into an ideology? If these hurdles are passed, does the Protestant consensus-religion these critics want have a substance different from that of mere secularity—is it more than a form? What is its generating center? Until this type of question is asked and answered, the pious criticisms of secular public schools and Supreme Courts remains beside the point, merely formal.

There are resources in Christian thought for relation to the patently secular. Devotion to these is more productive than are rehearsals of discomposure over the decline and displacement of Protestantism in national life. While it would be hazardous to develop a systematic theology out of St. Paul's word in Roman 13, that chapter at least illustrates the Christian intention to make its way positively in a non-Christian society.

St. Augustine pointed to a *natura* that was a potential for God's working both for the City of God and the City of Man. In the City of Man it was not of avail to the unregenerate person in his quest for the heavenly city. But God worked through it for the good of man also in pagan Rome. In the Reformation period, one strand of thought accented the *justitia civilis*. In the state this was again of no avail to the unregenerate person in his quest for a gracious God. But this civil righteousness was also God's instrument to man for doing good to man. In no sense was the Christian

Gospel related to this righteousness; it could belong to the pagan prince if he ruled justly; that is, if on the level of law there was a congruence with God's Law. The ruler was to avert evil, praise the good, provide for the general welfare. In the nineteenth century various Continental and Anglo-American thinkers, beginning with F. D. Maurice, developed approaches to the modern world. This approach asserts the Lordship of Christ over the powers and forces which do not recognize that Lordship. The Christian is asked to share with God in his suffering and glory in Christ in the middle of the world. Beginnings have been made in this fruitful quest.

When the accent is placed on responsible Protestantism, when this religious community is asked to converse and co-operate with others, when each is asked to be faithful to its own vision and to share where sharing is possible—then defeatism over the displacement of Protestantism can disappear. In this light the discussion of pluralism can proceed in new freedom. It is not necessary to keep up appearances, to create impressions, to wear masks. It is not necessary for Protestantism to carry the whole weight, the immobilizing burden, and the guilt for failure in the past. We have suggested that pluralism has its own problems; that it is only with hazard that it is itself molded into a consensus-religion. There are other problems. A pluralism-consensus can become one more charter for mere competition of religious institutions. It can provide new respectability for the same old religious conflicts. It can fascinate into immobility the champions of the ground rules of dialogue. But it can also permit the faiths to be fair to their own vision; it can furnish new levels of contact; it can promote temporary, pragmatic alliances of the good and for the sake of man. The hazards of *Verzuiling* (the Dutch sociologists' term for the columnization of life), of isolationist parochialism in pluralist life, are numerous. But the alternatives can be even more problematic.

We have spoken of pluralism in a variety of ways. We have been concerned to see it as a characteristic, if unsatisfactory, way of speaking of the religious situation after a particular faith has been displaced from its monopolistic hold on culture. The term "pluralism" is entering common parlance, particularly since World War II. The four war years of world travel, of uprootedness; the widespread collegiate experience of "displacement" after the war; the increase of mobility in a technological society; the mass media; new curiosity and new willingness to encounter others; new articulateness in the American religious communities; the religious revival of the 1950s—all these created the necessity for a term to describe religious life, and "pluralism" had to suffice. It is not ordinarily used in a precise philosophical sense. Ordinarily "pluralism" means nothing more than the ground rules: any number can play in America. In the eyes of others (Christopher Dawson is typical), it is an inaccurate term which screens our real secularism. That this "pluralism" inevitably permits the development of secularity alongside the distinctive religious witnesses is obvious. But the more the term is unburdened of philosophical connotation, the less pluralism (i.e., the phenomenon itself) serves as an ideological base, the more matter-of-factly it is regarded, the better it wards off such dangers. It is the most convenient term for a nation that has lost the innocence "placed" Christianity gave it.

Protestantism can serve to prevent the reality of pluralism from becoming a secular state Shinto. Theological resource is necessary to prevent the development of metaphysical sanction for the pluralist ground rules and dialogue. It can resist the development of pluralism as one new sophistication of the universalist, "After all, we are simply in different boats heading for the same shore." It must be aware that campus pluralism can be a corollary to, and agent of, relativism: everything is true, so nothing is true. This attitude cancels the moral and theological quest. Protestantism must resist the idolization of "process"—like Pascal's dancer concerned with where to put his feet, the dialogician talks ground rules without making a start at saying something. Protestantism stands to lose most if pluralism becomes the American Shinto. Jews have an ethnic base, Catholics have symbolic and canonical identities and hierarchical authority, which would protect them. But Protestantism would again blend into the wallpaper.

One further alternative is often offered besides existing faiths, historic generalized religion, or the newer pluralism raised to religious status. This is the development of a universal religion. In such a religion, the argument goes, the faiths which have had to yield cultural ground, to give up their place, would also give up their identities. They would contribute each what is best in its own particular past toward a new universalism. This was the suggestion of Franklin Baumer in the last chapter of *Religion and the Rise of Skepticism*. The suggestion is renewed by J. Paul Williams in a revised edition of *What Americans Believe and How They Worship*, and again by the suggestion of Deane Ferm in two articles in *The Christian Century*.[5] The same suggestion is implicit in Arnold Toynbee's championship of a syncretistic faith. The idea constantly reappears on the American soil that is so congenial to rationalist and natural religions which bask in the afterglow of historic religions. The problem with any such universal religion is also obvious. In addition to carrying the liabilities to which pluralism is prone as it becomes a religious idea, a universal religion must be given content and substance. And there is the truly insoluble nub problem. The moment a man sets out to devise a universal religion—usually through interreligious eclecticism—he comes up with something that is more particular by far than the historic religions, which must deal with the jagged edges of their respective revelations and the embarrassments of their history.

The defense of pluralism on these pages should not be taken as a defense of meaningless pluralism. There are no merits per se in *Verzuiling*, in a columnizing of life. Such a move could lead to but one more form of "placed" Christianity, out of contact with the world of man around it. Pluralism seen as a ground rule is needed only to protect existing authentic independencies. On a worldwide scale it provides the freedom for the intra-Christian ecumenical movement. It opens the question but does not provide the answer. Christian ecumenism is a separate problem, unrelated to interreligious and nonreligious pluralism.

Part Two

The World of

the Displaced Christian

6 CULTURAL AND SOCIAL DIMENSIONS OF DISPLACEMENT

THE LIFE of the displaced Christian seeks expression on two levels, in two arenas. One is in the world, in public, away from the resources of religious strongholds. The other is in the church, in private and in public, where he can draw immediately on the resources of gathered Christians. In the age when Christianity's cultural space is threatened, the cultural and social or public dimension of his expression will be changed decisively. He must therefore try to understand the dynamisms which relate to culture in this new setting. Most Christians seek to make most of their impact on the world through the church, particularly through the local church. But the public gets its notions of reality from images, pictures, impressions, media, in public life.

Why should the displaced Christian care for the world which has assaulted his claim to a place under the sun? He cares partly for historic reasons. His experience is nothing new: displacement was part of the original vision of the faith. The world that edged Jesus Christ out of the world had had no place for him. Jesus wept over this world, scorned its principalities and powers, faced its injustices, shared its agony, drank the cup of its death to the dregs. He also loved it and gave himself for it. The church as his body and each displaced Christian as a member of that body is called to exist for the world: to serve it and to carry on a Christian mission in it.

So that he can serve the world, the Christian wants his claims to be taken seriously. He is exposed to the world in many new ways today. He will be watched, and the more Christian his way and his witness appear, the more curiosity he will evoke. He represents (insofar as the faith takes on a cultural side) a partial culture inside a whole culture. Before he undertakes the task of relating the two he is inclined to ask the question not only of history but also of the future. Is there hope for his venture? When the world yielded ground to Christians, when there had been a place, the answer was simple: Christianity could tower over the environment and in many ways shape a culture.

Today, when there is in the world less and less sense of Christian civilizations, Christian nations, what happens to this cultural dimension? Will the believer be involved only in occasional raiding parties from the centers of Christian strength? Can he risk life, unprotected, at the side of the worldling? As these questions come up he is unconsciously and sometimes consciously asking questions of might and power. In the dynamics of relating faith and culture he is asking, Can a Christian culture prevail?

The outsider does not ordinarily ask this question. He does not need to. He may ask it in local situations, as a matter of self-defense. A Christian nativity scene on the courthouse lawn is to him a sign of Christian culture, offensive in a public setting. But in the world's larger situation, the nonbeliever is bored with this whole idea. He has already dismissed the cultural vitality of the Christian hunger artist. He has no interest in the one who has no taste for the food and no relish for the life of the world. He has moved on to the panther, which symbolizes the competing cultures and anticultures. They are full of excitement and promise.

It must be admitted that few Christians ask the cultural question consciously. Ordinarily they are content if they have religious freedom and a successful church life. If the Sunday School pictures are acceptable, the stained glass pretty, the Christian political expression innocuous, all is well. Yet the unspoken questions are often the more profound. Students of religious philosopher Paul Tillich report the convulsions that swept the classroom when, at the beginning of a seminar on ontology, the good professor would ask something like, "What child of six has not asked, 'Where do I belong in the structure of being?' "[1] But the professor was correct and the class was wrong. The child does ask that question. He asks it in other forms: What is behind the sky? Where did I come from and why do people die? How did bad people get to be bad if God is almighty and God is good?

So with the cultural question. It, too, usually appears in other forms: Why doesn't everybody like America? We are liberal, we give foreign aid, we brush our teeth, we are good Christians—why do the new African nations resent us so often? Why can only a Protestant look bigoted on the American scene? Why cannot public school children read the Bible—isn't this a Christian nation? Why is modern art's picture of Jesus so ugly? What is the Christian Democratic Party? I sent my daughter to a Christian college; why do they teach such unchristian ideas there? Why don't preachers stay out of politics? What business does a Christian World Order conference have talking about Red China? Why should atheists have rights? All these relate to the undergirding question: In the world of secularity, can a Christian culture prevail?

Many Christians are actually wagering their destiny on some version or other of the answer. They have been told that a *Kulturkampf*, a battle for civilization, is going on between the Christian West and the atheistic Communist world. They have often listened to sermons on the evils of materialism and secularism. They are quite aware of the conglomerate of anticultural, nihilistic forces around them. They know that the church is experiencing an uncertain moment, and they are confused by the partial answer they get.

> Each torpid turn of the world has such disinherited children,
> To whom no longer what's been, and not yet what's coming,
>   belongs. [Rilke][2]

Can a Christian culture prevail? Churchgoers hear of population statistics which foreshadow a world in which the Christian voice will represent a small minority. They are told that when they entered the world it was nominally one-third Christian; they will leave it on the lines of present trends, one-sixth Christian. After how many generations will their faith be culturally trivial, a mere curiosity? They hear, on the other hand, bells ringing in the tall towers of Christendom, and from the balconies they hear boasts that in the Christian West the religious enterprise is doing well. In such a confusing situation, what signs are reliable guides to the future?

Can a Christian culture prevail? The first answer to be given is theological: Yes, of course it can. God in his freedom and grace can work surprises. He can effect the unexpected. But in this book we must deal with current culturally documentable possibilities. The church can calculate only in the light of existing contexts. Its thought patterns and its strategies cannot be based only on a dream world or on an apocalyptic pattern—that would be irresponsible. When we speak of the breakdown of Christendom's Catholic phase and of the Protestant episode, we are speaking of the tangible memories of historiography.

Yes, God can initiate something new. Maybe customarily the record of these nineteen or twenty centuries has been misread. Maybe in God's economy they do not represent a long span. Maybe this is just the trial run, the first start. Maybe, says the man of faith, we are the early Christians. Maybe in God's time-scale the Soviet-Sino persecution of the church is occurring at the relative moment where we conventionally placed the Neronic one. He who sits in the heavens can laugh at the pride of nations which think that their Christian soil is his only instrument in history. Maybe a universal Christendom is one day to be formed by his Holy Spirit in ways that are at present wholly unenvisionable.

Theologically, all these possibilities remain open as a reminder of God's Lordship. They keep Christians open to the changes for which history cannot prepare them. But this openness has nothing at all to do with responsible living. Most men of faith must leave apocalyptic detail to Joachim de Fiore[3] or the modern pentecostalists. God calls Christians to service in the real world. Someone must care about the dying and those giving birth, about hoes and seeds, icons and burdens, cellos and quilts, altars and parades.

Will a Christian culture prevail? Almost as assuredly as we could answer theologically that it *can*, we must answer "sociologically" that it will not. The present disposition of nations and powers does not admit the possibility. The competition of cultures and churches, the space now occupied by secularity, and the ground rules of pluralism do not countenance this option. This view may seem surprising in a book that is concerned almost wholly with considering the cultural responsibilities of Christians. I re-emphasize, however: one of the earmarks of the displacing situation is the inability of Christians who are consistent with their heavenly vision, to baptize and monopolize a culture. The alternative to cultural monopoly is not cultural irresponsibility or a new individualism. The Christian has a responsibility in, to, over, and around cultures which do not bear his name.

Will a Christian culture prevail? Frequently this question is discussed in such a way that to answer "no" would lead to apathy, anger, or despair. On the level of daily affairs, many Christians expect a one-for-one return, perhaps with interest, on their cultural investment. They reason: We build Christian colleges: should they not fabricate a Christian culture? We elect Christian legislators: should they not pass laws favoring Christians? We sing Christian songs: should not the national chorus of praise mark us in the world as Christian? We pay for expensive church buildings: should not this cause the artistic community to bow and yield place to us? Why can't everyone be like us? We are respectable and keep the rules.

Now, it is easy to satirize such questioners. It is more difficult and more creative to listen to them. Ordinarily they speak for the most earnest and devoted participants in the Christian community. Unless patient hearing leads to clear answers there will be real warrant for their reluctance to invest in the cultural dimensions of the faith in the future.

Equally common are sophisticated ways of demanding that a Christian culture will prevail. These ways are often evident, for example, in the campus setting. Here there is greater willingness to recognize the temporary validity and potency of the world.

Secularity is first defined, accorded independent status, feared and admired. Then the adherent of the Christian faith is asked to go to work on the culture. Sometimes he is instructed to judge the culture from a view of the superiority of Christianity's cultural answers. More often he is asked to be relevant to this autonomous culture. The intentions here are excellent, and are not far removed from some of the suggestions which will follow. But a real possibility remains that the mere assertions of "relevance" will complicate the relation of the church to culture.

Be relevant. This command and the attempt to obey it can reduce the Christian to being a sort of switchboard operator. He makes connections between existing vitalities; but who cares about the connecting cord? In the advertising cartoons a shouting man runs down the street pointing to a fire; his potential audience is engrossed in a Philadelphia newspaper which "nearly everybody reads." The man's noisy assertions of relevance go unheeded. He remains pathetic. Or, to borrow Joseph Sittler's picture:[4] the men hired to park automobiles in the multistoried parking garages of the cities become virtuosi, artists at finding the openings, the slots, the connections, and with finesse. But sometimes, surely, they look out the window down to the street where the barely competent drivers are part of the traffic; below, men are at least getting somewhere.

Merely to assert relevance, to make connections, to call attention, helps neither the Christian mission nor the Christian sense of service. In *Death of a Salesman*[5] Willy Loman was always at a loss to explain his neighbor's boy. He knew the boy never would turn out to be anything. Bernard, now grown, is packing his bags for a trip to Washington and he chats with Willy while packing. After he has gone, Willy finds out that the young man is going to plead a case before the Supreme Court. Old braggart Willy expresses shock: What do you know, he didn't even say anything about it! Bernard's father has the answer: "He didn't have to. He is doing it." Self-advertisement and the claims of relevance often appear to the world like a substitute for action; those who do act do not often have to talk about it.

The Catholic attitude on this subject goes somewhat deeper than does the Protestant search for relevance and interest in making connections. The Catholic attitude has the advantage of historical references to culture on more impressive scales than does Protestantism in its more rootless modes. In defending the idea or the reality of Western Christian culture, these three authors rightfully point to its virtues. They point to those wondrous moments—I believe they were often wondrous—when Christ's sphere and culture's sphere really interpenetrated, interpermeated each other and created a vital fusion.[6] These moments of Christian politics, art, science, philosophy, education, and vocation could well be cherished by more of today's Christians. A future which will see more ambiguous and tenuous relations between Christian faith and secular culture may imply the loss of some of the possibility of such moments, and may involve real risk for Christians. I agree with Catholic cultural defenders that life in the West today cannot be understood without reference to the monumental achievement of Christendom. Looking at the centuries when Christianity had its place, one can still see them as the matrix of many durable values. This was home. "You were born here," the "secularized" British soldier reminds the buddy billeted with him in a German church in Christopher Fry's *A Sleep of Prisoners*.[7]

Only in the matters of the present and the future, of understanding and strategy, do the proposals of men like Dawson and Maritain make us uneasy. In effect, they attach the future of civilization to the prospect of the resuscitating, or re-creating a Christian Catholic culture. The future of the faith itself begins to be subtly dependent on this imperial cultural solution. Further, this Catholic interpretation often fails to do justice to the validities of secularity. After all, most Christians profit and know they profit from the secular political solution of modern times. Similarly, modern medicine wtih all its assets would hardly be with us had science been forced to develop within the limits the church set for it. One could cite many instances where the "children of darkness" had more light than those who had called themselves "children of light," made better use of the *natura* God provided in the City of Man. Often they showed more civil righteousness than did the warring, coercing, exploiting sects of their own times.

The Catholic cultural solution demands that Christianity again be seen as a counter-kingdom occupying ground, holding a place. This solution would demand great energies which might divert Christians from other tasks. It seems to imply kinds of authority and coercion not now open to Christians. (Christopher Dawson does not, of course, take us down the many lines described here; I am trying to envision how his type of solution would practically involve other Christians.)

The question can be pushed one step further: *Should* a Christian culture prevail? When the environment was nominally Christian, believers knew it would, could, and should prevail. I have no wish to criticize their age's every response to the possibilities history then presented. At the same time, a critical rereading of history might prompt us to ask whether we really would be so much better off if, in the modern world, a Christian culture could be refashioned.

The medieval unity was not so unified as it is generally pictured; the synthesis was not so architectonic and neat. In reality, Christian culture is not so consistent as it looks in romantic distance.[8] Medieval people still did much of their day's work apart from specific reference to the meaning God put into their tasks. They fought wars seldom tempered by what the church called Peaces of God or Truces of God. They buried their dead without always asserting a fully Christian attitude toward death. They were often less articulate, more misguided than are many Christians who make their way in the non-Christian cultures of any day. Distortion of that reality comes about in part because nostalgia oversimplifies. The romantic attitude is exaggerated by man's desire to make a model out of a world that never was. It is given credence by the fact that the wealth, authority, and might of the church once produced monuments of culture which remain (cathedrals, liturgies, empires), while the common aspects of life have vanished from memory (outhouses, folk expression, feudal pettiness). Thank God for the troubadours; their sensuality is still inescapable in the poetry whose music contradicts the monotonous coziness of "the idea of a Christian culture."

If a Christian culture will not and perhaps even should not prevail, what should happen? We have ruled out both sectarian anti-cultural withdrawal and individualisms which care about salvation *from* the world but not about resurrected life *in* the world. Somehow the Christian faith must find cultural expression, and must find it in ways consistent with its own genius, bearing the shame and the glory of the wounded and risen Christ in the middle of the world. Christians must act with disregard for the consequences which this action may bring upon their protected name.

Christian readiness to risk will spring from a more disciplined, not a less disciplined, Christianity. It will necessitate a more informed, not a less informed, faith. It will require venturesomeness and more finesse than does the attempt to create a Christian culture or the mere assertion of relevance. Such a "risked" mode of life will find Christians seeking out many kinds of alliances with the people of the world, engaging in joint battle for the good of man. Christian and worldling alike can fight against shoddiness, superficiality, evil, and exploitation in church and world alike. Both bases of cultural expression can be brought under critical scrutiny. Not everything in life has to be forced into a Christian mold in order to be of service to the church or to need the church's service.

The Christian can operate with the real aristocratic attitude of true servanthood. There is no servility in such a stance. He knows that Christ has overcome the world and is its Lord. He knows that Christ works in the world in the hiddenness of the church. He knows that nothing shall befall him without God's care. The Christian, most of all, can judge, lament, and weep over the world's agonies, its failure to recognize where its own good lies. He can also be free to rejoice in the world's good fortunes. No longer does he view the world from a fortress, from the distance of a sacred place. He is called to go into it, impelled to be its servant. God is to be served and praised not in the fortress but out there in the City of Man. Both the humane and the scientific disciplines are open to him, and he must serve in them with an intense dedication that mocks the world. He leaves behind the pallidity and limpness which often characterize and mock the genius of the church.

The stance of the Christian is important. In the early church the urgency of the end-time and a nonhistorical view of salvation led many Christians to assert an aloof *superiority* over the culture of man. Theology, they implied, is the queen of sciences, and the rest of the world either does not count or must do the Church obeisance. The culture must become Christian or the Christian must have nothing to do with the culture. What has Jerusalem to do with Athens?

In the centuries of placed, settled Christendom, this stance was carried over though now it was often accompanied by a more winning attitude. The urgency of the end-time was less real and the historical understanding of salvation was growing on the consciousness of Christians. They were no longer aloof. They stood *at the side* of man in his cultural attempts. Theology became the handmaiden, the partner of the sciences, and would create with them. The culture had become Christian; church and Christianized world could work together to wipe out pockets of resistance and irregularity.

In the centuries after Christendom, both attitudes recur. Superiority and aloofness are asserted in sectarian withdrawal. They are also present in the kind of *Verzuiling* (the attempt to develop a columnized Catholic life): Athens and Jerusalem have much to do with each other if both will first move to Rome. Parity, handmaidenhood—these survive in the Protestant quest for relevance and the Catholic revival of the idea of Christian culture. But the characteristic and effective stance now becomes *servanthood*. Christ gained his authority (Mark 10:42) not by being ministered unto but ministering. Theology, Professor H. Richard Niebuhr[9] avowed, is not queen but servant. The Christian accepts what God gives.

The believer then rejoices in creation's potential and agonizes over man's misuse of it. Christ is Lord of this creation, by whatever name it is called. The Christian moves in the world with freedom and responsibility. He seeks to help redeem the world, both through the words of those whose lives are "hid with Christ in God" and by his action and quiet service in his vocation. The Christian looks for new holiness in the ethical concern of the world, knowing that the Holy Spirit broods over the bent world. He knows that a

Christian's indifference and joylessness can become the new offenses which show the world his lack of faith. His faith, it is true, precedes the cultural intent: "Seek ye *first* the kingdom of God and his righteousness." But let him not be too busy to notice the inevitable corollary of life in the world: "and all these things shall be added unto you."

My hymn to the possibilities of Christian action in the world describes the stance and bearing. It does not describe the mechanism of cultural impact. This deserves considerable attention. There may be numerous ways or mechanisms of expressing relation. I shall present one full-length picture of what I find to be the best approach. This is based on an argument in *Evolution and Culture*[10] edited by Marshall D. Sahlins and Elman R. Service. The argument holds a curious attraction; ordinarily I find an approach through "laws" of cultural evolution uncongenial. (At the same time I would not wish to be taken as agreeing with Berthold Laufer of the Boas group that "the theory of cultural evolution [is] . . . the most inane, sterile, and pernicious theory in the whole theory of science . . ."!) In dealing with Sahlins' summary of two "laws" of culture, we shall see them merely as "historical observations." In that light they are less ironclad and less assertive in their pretense to prediction, and are also open to verification both by professional historians and by amateur observers. Sahlins states the "Law of Cultural Dominance" as follows:

That cultural system which more effectively exploits the energy resources of a given environment will tend to spread in that environment at the expense of less effective systems.

Applying that statement to our purposes, we shall begin by rearranging it. Remember that Christianity is not first of all a cultural system but a faith. But in the context of this book, systematic cultural capability of the faith is seen to be inevitable. Second, drop the word "exploits." The term carries semantic and ethical connotations and is unnecessary in our context. Third, recall that *our* "given environment" has some kinds of energy resources which do not lend themselves easily if at all to Christian relationship and use. In the historical sense, then, there is no danger lest this "Law

of Cultural Dominance" become a device for exploitation, a means
of introducing a pseudo-Christian or coercively Christian culture.
Theologically, Sahlins' "law" would apply only to those environmental resources which lend themselves to Christian expression. So
we restate this "law":

Whenever the Christian faith, insofar as it represents a cultural
system, makes more effective use of the energy resources of its cultural
environment it will tend to spread in that environment in more fortunate
relation to less effective systems.

To illustrate: Many of the nineteenth-century fraternal orders
(Freemasons, Oddfellows, etc.) presented intact cultural systems.
These were often based on ethnic, tribal, and class appeals that
have little force in the newer, open society. The obvious time-wast-
ing character of frivolous ceremonial became irritating to many
adherents. The leisure patterns of urban America changed: no
longer did "lodge night" call the male away from the family;
today couples look for opportunities to be together. Service clubs
have taken the place of the "lodges." With their brisk, efficient, fast-
paced noon-hour meetings, they appeal to the same gregarious
instinct and altruistic motives as did the earlier orders. But they
tend to prevail at the expense of the latter because they make better
use of the energy resources of a given environment. Illustrations
could be extended indefinitely, but then the reader can best profit
by fashioning his own and testing them.

Sahlins and his colleague approach formulation of their law not
through historical observation but by way of biological evolution.
They begin with E. B. Tyler's claim that evolution is "the great
principle that every scholar must lay firm hold of, if he intends to
understand either the world he lives in or the history of the past."
They quote Julian Huxley: "Evolution may be regarded as the
process by which the utilization of the earth's resources by living
matter is rendered progressively more efficient." They quote
Alfred Lotka who speaks in the same thermodynamic terms:
"Evolution proceeds in such direction as to make the total energy
flux through the system of [living things] a maximum."

Not that the process is unilinear. The authors remind us (quoting Herbert Spencer) that there is divergence and redivergence:

Each differentiated product gives origin to a new set of differentiated products. While spreading over the earth mankind have found environments of various characters, and in each case the social life fallen into, partly determined by the social life previously led, has been partly determined by the influences of the new environment; so that multiplying groups have tended ever to acquire differences, now major and now minor; there have arisen genera and species of societies.

Transferred to anthropology: a new cultural system soon becomes adapted and stable in its environment (Christendom in the West, in our book). It is seldom if ever displaced of its own volition. Usually external forces (here, secularity and the pluralism of the modern world) compel the system to give ground and seek new environments or new energy resources in the given environment.

Sahlins makes a useful distinction between culture as a closed system (general evolution) and culture as an open system (specific evolution). The distinction will also help forestall misreadings of the intention of this chapter. A culture may openly borrow, may derive, may be impelled by an ideology to "choose progress." "Has not the Christian religion, if not the Protestant Ethic, affected social and economic practice among many primitive peoples the world over?" Cultural systems have fewer ecological niches to fill than do biological systems. Thus their rise and spread is increasingly more dramatic and rapid. (Western culture, in its technology, dominates not only much of this planet but attempts also to dominate outer space.)

Sahlins' own full-length illustration of his "law" comes from the Great Plains of the United States. The specialized equestrian hunting culture of the Plains Indians made better use of the environment's energy resources than did the nearby agricultural systems. It held its own. But later, the practitioners of a more efficient agricultural system did displace the hunter.

From the standpoint of Euroamerican culture, the Indians' exploitation of the continent's rich resources was deemed to be highly inefficient and there was no question but that they had to go.

The tribes tried to copy Euro-American ways but they were too slow. Indian cultures were *not* uprooted in the Southwest where energy resources were considered low (Japanese were relocated there in World War II, and later on atomic bomb tests were held there). Concludes Sahlins: once all nooks and crannies of environment have been filled, a cultural system adapts and stabilizes until external pressure or a new dominant culture comes along. Thus the new nations of today advance suddenly but not without borrowing technology, modern weapons, or "the Protestant Ethic." "These societies give the impression of being built like the famous houses in *Gulliver's Travels,* from the roof down." They take the tools of adaptation from an already efficient and dominant system, to use them against their own earlier systems.

Paralleling this "Law of Cultural Dominance" is the "Law of Evolutionary Potential":

The more specialized and adapted a form in a given evolutionary stage, the smaller is its potential for passing to the next stage.

Again, it must be remembered that citing them does not imply acceptance of all the suspect and tenuous aspects of "cultural evolutionary laws." We are mindful of both theological and historical possibilities unenvisioned by such laws. But again this second law too can be translated with some confidence into historical observations. Here the mobility of the disciples of Jesus can be seen in context. Traveling light, without the baggage of scribal detail and Pharisaical law, they were able to pass into a "next stage." The Greco-Roman world was most ready for Christianization wherever the earlier civilization's energy resources had spent themselves. (That it was ready is seen even in Gibbon's tendentious observations about the decline and fall of Rome.) Where there was still some vitality in existing specialized forms, the new faith had more difficult going (Paul's general failure at Athens).

In connection with this passage into a "next stage" appears what Sahlins calls "the leapfrogging of age by youth," which has led to the cult of youth in dynamic cultures such as the United States, Russia, and China. In this connection, too, the "merits of cultural borrowing" (Veblen) and "the privilege of historical backwardness" (Trotsky) are evident. Here we note the weakness of the monuments and residues of placed Christianity in nonvital Christendom. The Protestantism of nineteenth-century America evolved into a twentieth-century form, so adapted and specialized, so at home in each ecological niche and nook, that it bore small potential for passing to new stages (e.g., a stage in which Christianity relates to secularity in new ways).

What does all this mean for Christian strategy? If there is any truth at all to these observations concerning characteristic ways in which cultures change, the lessons should begin to be obvious. If Christianity is content with the niches and nooks, the adapted and specialized places it found in the era of Christendom, it can continue to be custodian of its own cultural museum. There are virtues in antiquarianism, aestheticism, conservatism. They provide not wholly uncreative ways to spend the time until a final cultural displacement occurs.

If Christianity wants to participate in the forming of new cultural possibilities in a revolutionary world, however, it will have to "travel light" and yield up certain aspects of its adapted and specialized forms. Christian institutions, ministries, images, effects, must be studied: Which are very important? Which are accidental and can be left behind? Where should believers fall back on the "historical backwardness" of their primitive theology and where should they look to the merits of borrowing from secularity? Careful, patient assessment of these possibilities is necessary.

The objective for Christians is not to prevail or to find a place. Nor may they aim at survival and continued existence in nooks and crannies. Their intention is to participate, to serve in the positive aspects of the development of whatever new cultural possibilities emerge. No particular wisdom is needed to see the low-efficiency relation of much of today's Christianity to the energy resources of its environment. Christian institutions have related themselves well to certain elements in the adapted and stabilized culture. In a revolutionary world some believers have sought only escape and illusion. They want to be screened from the reality of the world's change and its needs; they want the institutions of the faith to enclose them in a shell, to sanction their prejudices and soothe their anxieties. In the years of the "Peace of Mind" cult (in the 1950s) American Christians often catered efficiently to the energy resources of this environment. They were successful; but in the process they were reduced to sharing niches and nooks with the least vital elements in a revolutionary world. Those who want to participate in the dynamics of a changing world are merely bored by the inefficient thermodynamics of such adaptation.

The whole statistical impulse of Christians to impress, the whole architectural façade of institutionalism must be seen in this light. A priest in a wealthy Chicago suburb has $1,500,000 to spend for a new church. He erects a monumental stonepile that underlines the irrelevance of Christendom. He tells reporters that he is thankful he is in a wealthy community so that he could afford to "build Gothic" and didn't need to build "modern." The newspapers devote one-eighth of a page in their Saturday afternoon edition to the dedication of the building. Never again does it "make news" or raise interest or questions or provide answers. The parish settles down to the unexciting task of spending twenty years paying for the pastor's pride. No one passing the church need feel challenged to think what Christianity might mean for his own day. The settled esthetic sensitivities of the existing parish are equally undisturbed.

Meanwhile, in postwar Germany Christians scrape up the rubble. They secure the service of a great architect, Otto Bartning. They erect *Notkirchen,* emergency churches. Possessing intrinsic charm and warmth, the inexpensive churches have great architectural interest. Whoever sees them is forced to think through questions of rubble and resurrection, Christian humility and witness. The suburban church involves a low ratio of yield on the energy resources of its environment; the *Notkirchen* involve an extremely high one.

A suburban church spends $300,000 a year to keep its program going. It air-conditions ninety classrooms so that children will be comfortable one hour a week. It buys expensive mail-order art for the lounge rooms. Its social life challenges the country clubs. The cultural environment is hardly challenged, changed, or improved. Meanwhile, in the inner city a store-front church spends $30,000 in a year. Some of the money goes for heat, light, and literature. A good bit more goes to help people fight rent gougers, to improve their living, and, on occasion, to eat a real meal. The suburban church represents a low efficiency in the thermodynamics of relation to environment; the store-front church, a high one.

A large convention of laymen in a denomination in annual meeting passes the usual resolutions underscoring the American Way of Life, criticizing foreign aid, investing in its own programs. But a student group on a campus discusses the relation of the faith to the lives of a number of participants who will take their place in the Peace Corps. Again a large church body spends great sums to build "separate but equal" college facilities for Negroes in the South. Meanwhile, eight college students engage in a sit-in in the name of Christ, for the sake of exploited fellow members of their race. In each of these pairs of examples, the higher efficiency in relation to the environment is found in the student groups.

Let us be clear about what these casual illustrations try to show. They do not suggest that the only thing the church does is seek to impress with great art, with ministry at the crossroads, with service to the exploited. The church ministers in many situations of quiet faith and nonfaith: at birth and in illness; to celebrate family joys and to keep the vigil; to tell children the Story; to provide a coherent view of the universe. But as far as the cultural question is concerned, a different set of factors must be involved.

The people of the environment have legitimate numbers of anxieties and complacencies which must be ministered to. The church need not be the only minister, but it must be a minister. Failure on the part of Christians to locate these energy resources in the environment leads to the cultural and social irrelevance of the church. They add to its theological displacement and contribute to its decline. In the short range they may be successful in their display. In the long range the intuition of the world locates the spot where the believers' real heart is.

This thermodynamic view will mean different things for every Christian. It will not mean that people in denominations and cells and congregations sit down January 1 each year and ask: "To what resource in the environment can we attach ourselves, in order to attract the world's curiosity?" Just the opposite. There was and there is a providential congruity between what the world needs and what Jesus Christ would offer as he stands at the world's side and ministers. Reading the newspaper (for awareness of the environment) and reading the Gospel (for awareness of the Christian impulse) will become full-time occupations of "the displaced Christian." This is no success formula. It does not guarantee that Christians will be able to "rejoice in this, that the spirits are subject to [them]" (Luke 10:20a). But it does mean that theologically, culturally, socially, their Lord must again be reckoned with, even by those who do not acknowledge his Lordship.

So far we have related the question of public Christian expression mainly to the cultural realm. The social field deserves separate attention. What is the impact of rapid social change on the church of the displaced Christian?

Some would say: Begin with the nonimpact of social change. We have already referred to what Gordon Allport calls "pluralistic ignorance." The in-group is self-preoccupied and measures the importance of the whole phenomenal world by what is important to itself. It is unaware of change around it, unable to cope with change. We have looked at the studied attempt by some Christians to foster illusions within their groups, to create artificial barriers to, and distances from, the dynamism of change. We have spoken of the frequent evidences of their ignorance, accidental or intentional; of the illusions and masks which a social group may nurture, the bravado it may put on in order to create a bandwagon effect. In all these circumstances social change can be screened out or reinterpreted to the group's liking. We are told by sociologists and church-planning experts that Christian congregations making sociological self-studies often cheat on the statistics they collect. The statistics are gathered only to help themselves appraise their mission. But in the face of community change, churches often distort their findings in order to justify obsolete but comfortable forms of ministry. In all these ways the milieu can be hidden.

We have spoken, secondly, of the impact of the church on social change. This impact was evident in the days before Christendom, when the world was being turned upside down. It was especially evident during the years when Christian culture occupied ground and took the larger responsibility for informing or governing a whole society. It remains an option after Christendom wherever the Christian ministry risks itself for the world without considering what this means for the church. Where this risk does not occur the church is seen to be a dependent variable. It reacts and adjusts and adapts in response to the prior changes in society. Thus it is always safe and secure.

The quest for security leads to the reason for the nonimpact of the church. As a power bloc the churches are, of course, still reckoned with in social life in Germany, Italy, and elsewhere. They may be a factor in the formation of political parties. In the United States, if they are sizable, lobbies in Washington see to it that the clienteles they represent have their way, or at least are not offended and alienated by the government. Those responsible for mass media know it is unwise to offend certain classes of religious people. Religiousness must be reckoned with—religiousness in the sense of the "sacred notions" (Joseph Fichter's term) which over-arch distinctive religious witness. But in concrete decision the actual content of the Christian faith need hardly be considered.

We are most interested, however, in a fourth option: the impact on the church of social change wherever it does occur. Despite attempts on the part of the faithful to ignore or create illusions, the psychic damage done by a mobile world dramatizes to Christians all kinds of signals, some of which evoke intense memories. The signals are dealt with somewhat differently in the varying situations. In Christendom they had to be appropriated for the sake of the action which might ensue because of the Christian responsibility for action. Today they sometimes awaken minority response. At other times they seem so potent they are dismissed as a cause for despair. That some of all this social change bears rich promise for the church was illustrated by the great modern drama of religious liberty, separation of church and state, and voluntaryism. In that instance social forces tended to dominate and in the end were welcomed by Christians.

In many respects, Christianity as a force has lost some of the mechanisms by which it was once able to protect itself from social change. Students of the psychology of affiliation note at least three

factors which build the kinds of loyalties that protect groups. First
are the positive attractions based on profound friendships. This factor tends to disappear, despite gregarious and communal impulses
in church people, because of today's mobility and technical society.
People move too often to become well acquainted; and in a technical society religion becomes one of the leisure pursuits of life, where
many of the less profound decisions are made. Often only the
casual, more tangential aspects of lives touch—not the aspects
where profound friendships grow, or where protection is formed
against alien signals. Most Christians' lives are exposed to the
world, apart from time spent with the religious institution. The
"Sunday morning problem" involves them in a split-level world; in
church words suddenly take on different meanings, a sense of un-
reality pervades the atmosphere, and the signals of the week are
forgotten.

The second affiliative factor which protects groups from social
change is threat coming from outside. The once widely preached
doctrine of hellfire (if it was believed) was such a threat. Excommunication, which ostracized the individual in the static, placed
Christian setting of the past, was another. But where most Christians have no lively fear of eternal damnation and are able to relate
easily to other Christian cells (or do not fear dissociation from
any), it is harder to develop the complete insulation needed to
screen off social change.

Another protective factor is restraint from within. In the days
when a person spent a lifetime in intimate contact with the same
local unit of Christians, this often required heroic effort. The dis-
approving visage of Aunt Marie in the church balcony was likely
to evoke more restraint than the presence of Yahweh. Today, restraint is imposed (or experienced) in the form of personality interests and subtle social forces. The casual character of affiliation
and the interchangeability of loyalties today operate against the
church's developing completely protective patterns.

What strategies are open in the world of the displaced Christian,
in the exposed society? They cannot depend essentially on removing
the impact of social change. There are, of course, isolated situ-

ations where this impact can be rather carefully planned and controlled. A child must organize his personality. Part of this process involves developing an organic world or universe around him. This can be done only with great difficulty "out there" in the world of complete exposure to a dialogical society, with its confusion of signals of social change. The child needs a place to stand to view the world. The church as a nursery carefully provides this place though it must be equally careful not to use the insular situation to provide illusions.

The adult also can legitimately see in the church a center where he can temporarily withdraw from some aspects of cultural and social impact. The human if he is to remain sane dare not tolerate the constant exposure of all his nerve endings. The body grows a cuticle to protect and organize its responses. Adult Christian education can provide some of this protection and organization, as it does whenever it asserts the priority of the theological over the sociological reality.

There can thus be some buffering, some reduction of shock. But Christian strategy does not concentrate on this. It looks for the theological potential in social change. The Christian believes that God works in the realm of culture's potential, in the civil righteousness of his servant in the state. Christians also need to seek discretion to form the proper alliances. All the resources of the long history of civilization—not only Christian but Greco-Roman, Euro-American, and now even Asian—are at hand to help them sort out good change from bad. Unconscious alliances church people form accidentally with elements in culture tend to be superficial and ultimately contrary to Christian intention. Conscious alliances and the proper building of bridges open up better opportunities for joint service of man by church and world alike.

The educational ministry of the churches can be devoted more conscientiously than it usually is to the real world. Such devotion does not imply the neglect of Biblical and doctrinal resource, but it does imply their connection with a world of social change. One glance at the Sunday School literature of most denominations will suggest the world of illusion in which they operate. Picture: an impossibly immaculate boy and girl, in a room with all toys on the shelves, listening to father read Scripture while mother adoringly looks on—a setting for a Family Altar that is improbable and perhaps not even salutary. Pictures of children approaching Jesus always show them among lambs and lilies. Their church is always an architectural model. Occasionally, to suggest liberality of racial outlook, an illustration will include a well-scrubbed Negro or mannequin-type Oriental young lady. The Sunday School lessons, as a glance at many curricula will show, ordinarily deal with the cozy aspects of minor virtues in the pattern of middle-class respectability. Many denominational family periodicals are just as remote from social change. When they print an article which verges on the controversial, it is often kept from really looking risky by the company it keeps on the journals' pages.

Those responsible for the churches' educational patterns can choose to deal with a real world. They can provide coherent views of this universe. They can reckon with those "portable" aspects of Christian theology which will equip Christians to face change in an overadapted, overstabilized culture.

Not all churches are located at the crossroads of cultural and social change. Perhaps the historic identification of Christianity with the West will mean that militant newer cultures will first have to negate an era, dismiss the faith. In the economy of God a whole portion of the church in a whole era or place may have to be written off as far as its ministerial potential to the world is concerned. It may be that the location of many churches within the Western middle class will mean alienation from the laboring classes, the disaffected races, or the intellectual and financial elites. Perhaps a generation will have to pass before the word can be effectively spoken to bridge the chasm. The signals churches emit may be so conditioned by the inhabitants of the gadget-laden paradise who receive them that their impact is blunted.

When such things happen, what is called for? The churches can minister in quiet ways to the inner needs of the flock that has already gathered and remains faithful. They can wait and prepare for a day when they are located again where they can serve on a large scale. They can practice the small-scale virtues in their own villages, yards, and kitchens. Most of all: their people can think and observe, act and speak, in such ways that they do not complicate the mission, witness, and service of those who are located where the environment offers more resources of energy to the Christian Good News.

7 CULTURAL AND SOCIAL EXPRESSIONS OF DISPLACEMENT

T HE DISPLACED Christian finds numerous public as as well as private outlets for expressing his faith. In the cultural and social spheres his imagination can be exercised in the fine arts, the university, the public media, in social action and ethics—both public and personal. His forefather could do the same, in a somewhat more compact and apparently less chaotic universe. To the forefather, the gallery was always open: the church was the chief patron of the arts. Secular subject matter was largely dismissed and was at best the occasional guest. The earlier university's universe was in some senses the self-contained world of Christian vision, though this situation did not last long. In the age of groundholding Christendom the public media had not developed extensively, but the earliest forms (e.g., the printing press with movable type) were naturally instruments for its service. The action of the Christian prince came under a different kind of ecclesiastical scrutiny than it now would.

All this is changed. A Christian artist may still work for the church and deal with Christian subject matter. There are Christian universities, but the intellectual assumptions and commitments of their professors and students are more complex than those of medi-

100

eval schoolmen. The public media are rarely dominated by Christian expression. The idea of the Christian state is an anomaly in the modern setting.

The churches can therefore decide to abandon their whole cultural involvement in each of these departments of life. They can leave the world to its own devices. Sometimes they are counseled to build no bridges to the world's culture. Sometimes, nevertheless, they recover an acreage of lost ground. Now and then, here and there, they take captive one of the media of expression (e.g., a religious radio station). Circumstances sometimes permit explicit Christian political behavior. Often Christians are urged to compartmentalize: to be private Christians and public agnostics, making no attempt to relate their inner worlds; or, again, to plunge and immerse themselves in the secular realm and let the faith, as a private domain, take care of itself. Sometimes they are even told that in the cultural realm the odds are so overpowering one should surrender all at the outset.

How does Christianity in its displaced setting seek and get a hearing? Some decisive illustrations can point directions.

We have said that the Christian's imagination can be exercised. What is the rootage of Christian expression in the imagination today? Up to now, in this book, we have been staring the sociological facts in the eye, trying really to see them on their own terms and to let some of what we see become part of our consciousness. But the Christian is not a camera of values, he is also a projector.

The Christian imagination in a time of displacement will organize its world in different fashion than when it was custodian of virtually the whole cultural possibility. From the religious viewpoint, the imagination is located in work and discipline, in belief, in relation to a community, and to the concrete world surrounding the Christian.

Difficult homework faces the Christian creator. He cannot evade his working at perfecting his craft—now less than ever. He, too, has an eight- or sixteen-hour day. The finger exercises, the academic drawing lessons, the arts of politics, must be his discipline— his most of all because revolutionary elements in the culture will not be predisposed to listen to him. As a representative of what they have dismissed and found obsolete or unexciting, he must master a double measure of excellence in the craft.

Is this the basic problem? Do Christians in their use of public forms of expression lack technique, virtuosity? Is it not rather, to recall Flaubert, "the thing itself"[1] that is lacking—the melody, not the bowing technique?

That the Christian imagination should seem to many so dulled and relaxed is difficult to account for, unless by the sense of insecurity resulting from displacement. The museum curator guards his ancient objects: he is not expected to provide expressionist paintings to hang on the wall. Nothing, I am convinced, will do more to awaken the Christian imagination than to reverse the defeatist images of Christianity as mere conservator of values in Western civilization. No one will give much attention to Christians if they are nothing more than conservators. New dominant cultures will not conserve, they will borrow and exploit living elements of Western culture. The theological, social, and cultural visions which relate the Christian faith to a pluralistic and secular world represent a more vivid challenge for the imagination. The song in the chaos of the oppressed Negro soul gave birth to the art forms of the spiritual and jazz. The parable of urban alienation furnished the substance for a whole generation of Jewish fiction writers who attracted a nation's attention. Only an occasional Christian mutation can impress the culture if the basic vision be the obsolete concern for Christianity's good name and settled place under the sun.

Joining the exiles, the displaced, the strangers, joining the human race and the pilgrim march of Christians, offers the artist better possibilities. The excitements of this age are manifold. It was the Oriental wise man who prayed the gods to keep him from living in an interesting age. But both Oriental and Occidental creators have no choice now but to cope with an interesting age. Tedium, ennui, may characterize the society concerning which the artist writes or paints. But to the "wise man," the manifoldness of that world provides more possibilities than more unified cultures could.

The Christian imagination is rooted in belief. The presence of unbelief under the forms of religious institutions is certainly one factor limiting Christian expression. Might it be that the widespread nostalgia for settled and placed Christianity represents a cultural cover-up for radical unbelief or a spiritual vacuum? Does the defensive modern Christian expect a conservative cultural setting to provide a coherent view of the universe when his own faith is shallow? Even a canvass of that possibility might be the occasion for works of Christian imagination!

In the stage version of Arthur Koestler's *Darkness at Noon*[2] this kind of problem is dealt with. Rubashov, the old revolutionary, is imprisoned as a deviationist. But he reminds his efficient second-generation purger, Gletkin, that his own, Rubashov's, generation really believed in the revolution, ate, drank, dreamed, hymned, loved, and died for the revolution. Gletkin belongs to a generation "born without a navel." Much of the defensive and conservative talk in the institutions of Christian civilization may represent this quest for roots where there are none, be a smoke screen for an absent faith.

To repeat: the absence of faith or the agony over threats to it relates to the Christian imagination. Institutional façades covering the absence only bore people. That is why the Christian artist may not always follow the conventional disciplines of institutionalized parish life. The Christian sometimes complains that the imagination is dulled and blunted by the low-keyed, small-bore protectionist view of the typical congregation. It is this same man of imagination, however, who, through the suffering caused him by such a misreading of the Christian faith, could aid and support his settled contemporaries when they do face the issue.

Another aspect of Christian imagination called forth by the time of displacement is rooted in a relation to community. Real communication goes on, according to Karl Jaspers,[3] only between those who share a basic belief. The Christian artist stands between the Christian community and the secular world. Vocationally, he is called to deal with the language and aspirations of both. Hopefully, he brings the two somehow together under his own witness to the Lordship of Christ.

Here again the parable of displacement which has obsessed artists and poets for the past few decades can be the artist's instrument as he jostles those who are comfortable in the settled life of post-Christendom. Where the change and insecurity of a community are profoundly recognized, there is material for exciting art. The whole school of chroniclers of the end of the old American South is a typical example of how cultural change can stimulate the creative man. Much of the most interesting cultural expression of religion at the moment comes from the American South, from South Africa, and from emergent Israel. In each case the clash between sociological and interpersonal dialogue, between barrier and interaction, between past and present, is most vivid.

Since the Christian, being no longer settled but now uprooted, makes his expression in a world of concrete experience, the Christian imagination must be more deeply rooted than ever before. When novelist François Mauriac called himself a "metaphysician dealing in the concrete," he located the place of the artist or ethical leader of the Christian community today. The artist gives flesh and blood to theological assertions. He speaks of the battlefields and the farmyards, the players and the wanderers, while theologians speak of sin and grace and sociologists of rapid change.

Unbelief, the absence of community, and abstraction—these are the enemies of Christian imagination, and they seem to be unrecognized. Suppose these enemies are defeated. Suppose the imagination is again present and vivid: how does the displaced Christian find expression? The fine arts endure as prime servants of an age's self-interpretations. To the real artist is given the ability to see, beyond the externals of the moment, the viscera and the heart of his day. Often he is just sufficiently out of step with the present that he anticipates a coming time. (From the poetry, of the past quarter century, we have derived the basic picture of "the exile" or the displaced person, even though the reality—on the universal scale—followed the symbol by some years.) The fine arts of our day witness to the disintegration, the uncertainty, the violence, the chaos, that accompany the coming of a new day. Not all of today's art forms immediately seem to lend themselves to use for bearing Christian symbolism. That they do not may in itself be a parable. Yet which medium of art should be ruled out? The abstract expressionist of painters and sculptors? Alfred Manessier does well with Christian themes in this violent world. Atonal music? François Poulenc, Hugo Distler, Messiaen, have not found the form uncongenial. Modern poetic forms? T. S. Eliot, W. H. Auden, and others are at home with them.

The artist experiences a doubly complex world. Not only is he alien and yet spokesman to the religious and secular community, but he must deal with the disintegration of the secular community. The existence of what novelist C. P. Snow calls two cultures—the scientific and the humanistic—presents a real problem to him. The humanistic culture itself is made up of disruptive elements: pluralism does not provide the coherent base for expression which a unified culture can offer. Yet the fine arts serve today to reveal much of the chaotic character of the world and to anticipate its future. The church turns with hope and sometimes with daring to the parable they set forth.

It is difficult to envision a real renewal of faith inside culture without a parallel renewal of Christian artistic expression. Before faith comes, Luther reminds us, there must be a knowledge of history. The artist reads the history of his own day in the light of the myths that hold his own universe together. He is the best warrior against the spiritualism, the Docetic abstraction from the phenomenal world, which is the defensive church's temptation. He celebrates a world which God creates, in which in Christ he is incarnate. In the suburbs and the garbage dumps of this world's Jerusalems Christ is crucified, and in its gardens and upper rooms and on its lakesides the resurrected Lord is known by the disciples. "Taste and see that the Lord is sweet." "Handle me and see." The artist reckons with the concrete order and calls the church to the world in which its mission and service are to be carried on and interpreted. He is called to do this with finesse: he dare not be like the student of dancing, preoccupied with where to put the feet; he must move. He cannot wait for the universe to hold still: he must depict the displaced life in the mobility of its occurrences.

Should one stress the priority of cultural expression today?

The fine arts do provide another instance where there is tension in the thought of the displaced church. How much treasure and energy dare go into the ecstasy and agony, the analysis and celebration, of cultural forms? Are not single-minded verbal formulas clearer, more efficient means of carrying on a mission to the world? Is it not through words that souls will be saved and bodies healed? No matter on what level the artist enters—whether he contends that art is grace, that art transforms creation, that art supports the means of grace or is at least positively related to them—his enterprise will be questioned in the name of Christian mission and stewardship.

The question could be to the displaced and disinherited Christian to whom belongs "no longer what's been and not yet what's here": how does his art (creation, belonging to the beginning) relate to mission (eschatology, belonging to the end-time)? Art celebrates the gift of God in the old creation; eschatology, the act of God in the new. Art envisions the life of man in the middle of the world; eschatology, the action of God at the end. Art represents the temptation of creative man to overassert his freedom; eschatology points singly to God's freedom. Art implies some kind of union with creation and its elements; eschatology witnesses to the highest dualism. Art points to the depth of human experience; eschatology points beyond human experience. Art belongs to the *chronos* of calendar time; eschatology belongs to the *kairos* of God's decisive, interrupting time. Art is catholic, endowing as do sun and rain the evil and the good alike; eschatology is selective: "the one shall be taken and the other left." In the time of disinheritance, Christians are often counseled to be missionaries of the end-time and not celebrators of the beginning or creative time.

The artist knows that he expresses himself between the two poles. He cannot listen to the eschatologist without leaving behind the positive interest and the eucharist of the Old Testament. He cannot listen to the mere celebrator without turning his back on the urgency of the New Testament, denying the missionary impulse to the fields white unto harvest. By his position he witnesses to the whole church concerning the double-sidedness of its ministry.

It must be admitted that two extreme temptations are present here to distract from the parable. The Catholic Christian, with more sense of place and enjoyment of the world, can easily become the aesthete who turns his back on responsibility. The missionary Christian, in his urgency, may turn his back on the redeemed dimensions of the world. He assumes that the only task of the church is its own enlargement, not nurture of its children; that eternal life begins somehow after death and has nothing to do with life; that the Christian mission means only the rescue of people out of God's created world. It is in this tension that the parable of displacement is most needed. The artist moves with real temporality and grace in the promised lands that never become his permanent property. He acts as if their color, shape, sound, belong to him. He guides the observer, listener, or reader through these lands with the sanity that the vision of the eternal city gives him.

When the artist creates something new out of the raw material of an age of Christian displacement, he shows that he is not abandoning the world. Abraham again is his father, as are God's singer, David, or God's builders, Ezra and Nehemiah. He is not captive of the intellectualism which reduces the whole life of the church to formulas ("Are you saved?" "Jesus saves.") He knows that God reveals in acting and showing as well as in words. He refutes the demythologizers of fundamentalist bent who find importance only in words about Jesus. He refutes the churchmen who too often criticize the modern world as a doctor does who censures the patient for using his eyes because his ears are stopped. He knows the dangers of monotonous verbalizing; "the freshness of being evaporates in mere repetition" (Whitehead). He helps the church sing the new song.

If his contribution is chiefly along the lines of the first article of Christian faith (creation), the artist is also called to stand between creation and eschatology in matter of the second article, the redemption of the world. The rabbi, told that the world is redeemed, looks out the window and says, "I do not see much difference." The artist sees; his task is to help others see (*schauen,* in Goethe's sense: really to see). But his approach is a refutation of what has been called a "soteriological anthropomorphism"—a Christianity that cares only about man in the act of being saved from the world. The church does not bottle the Christian in baptismal water and ship him off to mansions above. The artist celebrates the redemption that occurs along the journey. He is aware that history does not exhaust God's purposes for man but he does find that history important. He tells in detail who man is, who Christ is, from what and for what man is saved.

The artist's work is also related to the third article of the creed—the sanctifying signs in a secular world. The Spirit's brooding gives the human creator his charter; the Spirit's guiding gives him courage.

Most artists at work would hardly articulate their mission in these terms. Their task is to pursue their own crafts and sullen arts unburdened by too many theological considerations. But their half of Christian expression amounts to such an articulation. It is then for the missionary to place the artist's work into another perspective. Thus the mission takes on a new, winning character. Its vision is no longer limited to snatching men from the world. "Life in Christ received a horizon in place of a boundary" (P. T. Forsyth). With his

> good, mery
> glad and joyfull tidings, [God] maketh a
> mannes hert glad, and maketh hym synge,
> dance and leepe for joye [Tyndale].

The artist stands at the side of the missionary on that horizon. The impatient, restless, rootless age does not by any means dull the eschatological vision; but it most needs the artistic expression.

Art we shall have in any case. The only question is whether it will be good art or bad, complicating or helpful. Art is double-sided; it points to the aesthetic Davids, who in their song are described as men after God's heart. It points to the iconoclastic John the Baptists, who in turn will point fingers so long as there are Auschwitzes and divorces in the world. "A man will have to give account on the judgment day of every good thing which he has refused to enjoy when he might have done so," says the Christian too —even in a secular world where the Lordship of Christ must be asserted anew.

From the suspect world of the fine arts Christian expression moves to the world of the university, to intellectual academic witness. Like the artist, the intellectual stands between two communities: the circle of faith and the circle of inquiry. The university symbolizes the dialogical, intersectioned view of life. What holds the university together today is *not* the Christian faith or religion but nonreligion. This is only a little less true of Christian-sponsored schools as of their secular counterparts. Their laws, their codes of conduct, their chapel services, their religion classes, may be excellent arenas of witness and life, but the schools' real base in laboratory, classroom, and dormitory relates to the secular pattern of vitalities. The university has a different universe than it did at its birth in Paris or Bologna in the years when Christendom had a place.

But the nonreligious character of the university enterprise does not mean that the church can wait out or dismiss the campus years. It ministers to people where they are; first pastorally, and then in relation to their studies. It is unfortunate that the interest in restoring Christian places and occupied territory forces on the Christian universities and ministers the task of overadvertising their claims. (Usually, overexpectation is extended the undersubsidized expressions of church life.)

In the university the church must be content with small gains. The latent unbelief of a generation becomes patent and acute in the inquiring universities. And anti-institutionalism—suppressed in the child and comatose in the adult—finds expression, sometimes even creative expression, at the hands of the university student. The ethical lapses and cultural irrelevance of the church are faced most radically—if sometimes irresponsibly—during the campus years.

The church's vision of the university and the ministry is often distorted by false expectations. Campus disaffection is often read as ideological rejection of the church when it is in fact merely the result of lethargy. Many intellectual and social forces bid for the scholar's time, most of them with more coercive and persuasive power than the churches can muster. Many kinds of loyalties are sustained in the hiddenness of campus Christian witness. Above all, the university like the art gallery offers a glimpse of the way in which decision is reached in the world which follows upon Christendom's demise. A ministry of listening must precede a ministry of judgment there.

Equally complicated, and affecting vastly more people, is the expression of Christian faith in the public media. Here again it becomes clear how decision is reached, power recognized, vitality measured, in the contemporary world. The illusions of the American dormitory suburb and the quiet parish are dispelled. The media by their nature belong to the technical, secular world. Products of that world, they in turn help disseminate its assumptions. In a society with many religious elements and power blocs, the media take a respectful attitude toward religious interests. But "prime time" and front page seldom deal with Christianity's place in culture. When they do, in any concerned fashion, it is in relation to those expressions of the faith that are furthest removed from institutional religion—those which (to repeat the accent of the last chapter) give forth the highest efficiency in relation to the environment's energy resources.

The media do not have absolute power, of course. We all know the limits of art gallery and university in shaping the totality of life in a pluralistic world; but because of their pervasiveness we forget the limits of the media. While most men receive notions of reality from them, they do not do so from them alone. Failures of the churches in this realm need not prompt despair. Christian work in the world goes on, in, with, and in spite of media.

Christians tend to greet each technological change with exaggerated claims ("Preach in one day to more people than St. Paul did in a life time"), followed by disappointment ("But our polls show that nothing took effect"). There is cause for cheer in the fact that man has countermeasures; "man will prevail," he is durable. The media are only part of the revolutionary world. The root experiences of life are certainly more profound than anything the media can convey. A child may watch a thousand situation comedies of family life on television. They will not have nearly so strong an impact on him as will tension between his parents. Many social forces seem to have more determinative effects on the individual than the communications media. The approval of a group, the predispositions one brings to the media, the self-contradictory character of the communicators' claims—all serve to counter the influence of the media. The more profound one's ego involvement, the less conversionist impact they seem to have. Religion and politics represent high degrees of ego involvement; in these realms, students of the effects of communication suggest, reinforcement rather than conversion should be the aim of the communicators.

Having pointed to these limitations of the media, we must also recognize their potency to help displace Christian claims. For example, their tendency to cater to sensation without calling for commitment so dulls the viewer or reader's sense of responsiveness that he is likely to be deaf or indifferent to matters of ultimate interest. One cannot possibly buy *all* the kinds of toothpaste advertised or really care for all the heroes presented. Again, the amount of time consumed by the voracious media leads to a disproportionate sense of values. The American child who spends the average twenty hours per week in front of television and less than an hour in a low-keyed Sunday School setting will draw his own conclusions about the "place" of the faith in life. Further, the media tend to trivialize life—by extending rhetorical interest to many insignificant aspects of life, by soliciting involvement in so many self-contradictory features.

The world of secularity is complex; the media often oversimplify it and so create false pictures. Joseph Goebbels knew their power: "Whoever speaks the first word on a subject to society speaks the true word." The priority and the strident repetition open to the propagandist or the advertiser dull the discretion of the client. The media can confer false status on their own worlds of power; anyone who has listened to the chatter of certain kinds of newspaper columnists knows how falsely the importance of "in" or acceptable people can be measured.

Because they must appeal to a mass audience, the media are driven to select for presentation only certain aspects of complex realities, with the result that they convey distorted images of reality. Usually they are commercially based, and economic interests lead them to deal with apparently controversial affairs as though they were dealing with real controversiality. Almost every evidence of impact by the media complicates the Christian's sense of reality. He is asked to work in the complex, paradoxical, controversial world and still to minister in and through the world of the media.

What does the Christian do? Again, he welcomes the parables of displacement that he receives through the assumptions of the public media. They reveal to him how remote the self-contained ecclesiastical world is from the way importance is actually determined in the subway and on the farm. But the empirical studies which show man's resistance to the media give him courage. Of most of the complicating signals he can say, "This, too, will pass." The fads and fancies which distract one day are gone the next. He learns from the media how community is yearned for and sometimes created. The barrier between man and man is often crossed, if only superficially, by discussion on the part of two "expert" men on the street who have heard a baseball game, seen a motion picture star, watched an astronaut. To this world of groping interpersonality and pseudo-community the Christian must minister with a more profound kind of fellowship.

The believer recognizes the ways in which mass culture has given rise to new audiences and new instruments to face those audiences. He locates new environments and new energy resources in those environments. As he comes to understand and employ the media, he strives to create alliances with those elements in them that work for the good of man, whether in the name of Christ or not.

In this discussion we have no immediate interest in how the media are to be employed to speak to the Christian community. It is my impression that churches have been most successful here. But how are they to minister in the larger world formed by the media? The mass audience, for all its pluralism, does tend to develop a consensus and a language. Inevitably a "common faith" asserts itself, a national religion carrying memories of the Christian faith. These "sacred notions" serve as surrogates for historical and revealed religions. They make up the environment. It has its energy resources. They can be exploited ("Will Your Child Be Mongoloid?" screams the cover of a women's magazine) or understood.

In the realm of the media, as in realms of art and learning, it seems important that the right alliances be formed, since Christians do not have the field and the ground to themselves. The temptation to tie Christian witness to the sacred notions of the media is great. Secularity actually offers more potential: the religious *King of*

Kings can complicate Christian witness; the frankly worldly *La Dolce Vita* can jostle and clarify it. Elsewhere I have suggested in some detail how Christians might understand and employ the media —in general, in a way just the opposite of that in which the church ministers to its members.[4] In the Christian community, proclamation is normative, teaching secondary, and action the by-product or outgrowth. In the realm of the public media the church has a different problem. In relation to the post-Christendom environment, the preached word appears to be made up of slogans without reference or meaning; teaching is of more value; the parable or drama —action, service, ministry in real life or fiction—gives the highest and most efficient energy yield.

Different problems arise when the churches employ the media in the conscious task of "public relations." As they select elements in their complex life to present to the world, they inevitably engage in advertising. The relation of Christian thought to this venture needs separate attention. All moves of the church toward the world are public relations, good or bad. André Siegfried has called this the "age of publicity" and in doing so he pointed to another environmental factor with which the displaced Christian must reckon.

The church is a collective representation; it presents itself to other collectives and to individuals through public relations. Does this advertisement necessarily contradict the Gospel in that it calls attention to the church's self when humility is called for? Here, it would seem, what is decisive is the aspect of the self the church chooses to present. Christians know that it is incongruous to boast and to advertise pomp and power in the name of a dying Galilean failure. It is certainly heretical to call attention to the church for its own sake. But the church is asked to commend itself to men; preaching "not itself" does not mean it does not preach or relate its intentions. A self-critical discipline of public relations, located near the power centers of the churches and at the edges of the world's power centers, can play a decisive part in fostering understanding between the two worlds.

The function of public relations in the church is to present and represent Jesus Christ to its members and to the world. It will have to do this in a form consonant with his character: it must come as a servant and not as a queen. Advertisement must make clear its intentions. Sometimes it will interpret actions of the churches. Then, in a pre-evangelical sense, it will seek to awaken the larger community's curiosity and to commend the church's Lord. The mode of this presentation parallels that of education: it selects and organizes aspects of the effective world. The aristocracy of real servanthood after the pattern of Christ determines the manner. Such public relations asks the church and the world, "Come and see." It asks with Christ, in the middle of the world, "Watch with me one hour."

When the churches publish for anyone beyond their own clientele they encounter similar problems and opportunities. Marketing problems in reaching the larger public are great and present a separate category. At this point we are interested in the question of the substance of what is said. In this matter, too, the context is determinative. Whenever the Christian printed page is part of the self-defensive quest for a religious place under the sun it becomes unexciting to the world. The irrelevance of the denominational enterprise strikes those who come across the literature of denominations other than their own; the outsider finds it self-defeating and purposeless.

A study of the self-defensive literature suggests that most Christian aggression is actually too defensive. With the protection of the church in mind it inserts the fatal word "still" in its questions: "Can men still believe?" "Is the church still faithful?" "Is the Gospel still relevant?" (The answer, of course, is always yes.) The reader who recognizes the canker betrayed by the word "still" is not likely to look for vitality in such a setting. In the world of displaced Christianity those who fight for its place under the sun tend to answer questions which the society does not ask. The impulse in, for instance, American Protestantism to show that it belongs in America hardly answers the question, What do you have distinctively to say to America?

The pluralistic innocence of the churches shows up most frequently on the printed page intended for religious clients. In the religious press, application of the Gospel is often related to the scrubbed-up middle-class world that seldom comes closer to the

revolution of our times than do the characters in a soap opera. The
publications often find relief in contrived parables of "relevance."
The low state of religious publication in the United States is being
raised somewhat as the denominations merge. The literature of
these larger bodies tends to express a greater catholicity and daring. By no means all denominations' literature can any longer be
accused of shielding people from the social and cultural change
of the day.

The displaced Christian recognizes that the strongest (and original) base of a secular society is its laws and its political orientation. The displacement of Christianity in the West has led to the
development of states that makes their decisions with no reference
to divine revelation, as might be expected. Many of them, however,
sense a necessity to erect a deity in place of the departed gods.
This is modern nationalism, which commands ceremonial interest
and philosophical sanction. No matter: whether a state is technically religious or nonreligious in orientation, the result from the
Christian viewpoint is a masked secularity. The church therefore
is called to a critique of nationalism and national goals. Its contact
with the state is through its concern for God's law (and not through
the Gospel). This law demands the Christian summon the state
to a situation of care for the neighbor and carefulness in applying
that care.

In the secular world the churches are often misled by the state's
perfunctory religious affirmations. The theistic tokens in the founding documents of the United States of America may well be part of
that providential or at least fortunate combination of circumstances
by which Christianity, rationalism, nonreligion, and a practical setting conspired to produce a free society. But the slogan "In God
We Trust" and the phrase "under God" in the pledge of allegiance
of the United States flag offer too uncertain a base for alliance between concerned Christian and careful statesman.

The Christian who acknowledges Christ's Lordship over all of
life and who recognizes the civil righteousness in which God can be
at work does not need to ask the state to provide him with a Christian "place" in the world. He knows how to deal with things as they

are and to find kinships in a situation where the name of God is not carelessly and casually employed. He has the freedom just to be a man and a citizen, untrammeled by the ceremonials of nationalist religion.

Church and state can serve to check each other's tendencies to provincialism. The church as a universal fellowship should care about the whole world's resources, be concerned for mission to the whole world. As it turns out the churches often become overidentified with the local and national interest and are less equipped than the state to transcend national boundaries. Thus the practical situation of life in a shrunken world may force an internationalism on the nations. When the churches sustain imagination for the whole world's need, they are capable of pointing to goals which transcend those of the individual nation. They can do this through the hidden witness of Christian citizens, through lobbies and resolutions, through impact on statesmen, through their own international involvements. Christians located in nations that are not in a revolutionary situation can serve well to help the quiescent societies understand the nature and motives of revolution where it does exist.

The interplay of Christian and public servant can be creative in that each can provide a check on the other's tendency to abstract policy from life. The state proclaims great goals, sometimes at the expense of the person. The Christian can ask what the programs mean in detail, and can help see to it that the detail is carefully administered. The churches often assert an interest in all men, but their word remains on the level of abstraction. They cannot always, in the elites of power of a complex world, provide outlets for the concrete expression. But they minister to citizens who can find these outlets in the public world.

Churchmen and statesmen can bring checks and counterchecks on each other's readings of history. Robert L. Heilbroner, in his book *The Future As History*, points, for instance, to the American optimism which, while it is appealing, can be dangerous in a nuclear world. The Christian church, which should have learned from the history of its own displacement, ought to be first to recall the tragic sense of life: not everything in history turns out the way one wants it to. Such a sense can add to life a sanity which nations do not always show. When states presume to take history into their own hands (and issue such optimistic and boastful proclamations as "The thousand-year Reich," "America as God's footstool"), the churches can witness against them. The experience of displacement provides potentially a dialogue as creative as that between Pope and Emperor in the settled setting of Christendom's past.

Again, churchmen and statesmen can serve to check each other's failure to recognize human solidarity. The nation must be concerned about all the people in it and about the people in other states; thus it often shows a catholicity which the churches, looking after themselves and their place, do not show. The detailed opportunities the nation offers through ballot box, welfare, and social service can be instruments for Christians. On the other hand, the voluntary activity of the churches may often point to enduring personal needs in a time when the administration of welfare is automated and impersonal.

In those portions of the West where the terrain was once officially Christian, the officially secular states frequently have as much difficulty defining their situation as the churches have locating themselves in the states. Fruitful dialogue, participation, and real criticism between the two types of collective representations, churches and states, can proceed in a variety of forms once the nature of secularity is perceived and defined and the once-monopolistic intent of the Christian churches is shown to be broken down.

Of course, the chief interest of the churches will be in the ethical life of the states. They cannot avoid a concern that the detail be carried out, for a technical society's lack of ethics usually reveals itself in the details of its life and action. The churches are given no special discretion in this field. They are given a mandate, however, to see to the care for the neighbor. The Christian does not look only for voluntary or individualistic niches in a welfare society. He seeks to minister without regard for his place and name wherever there is need.

In the secular setting, the churches come once more not as queens but as servants. (The state, of course, would not and could not welcome any other form of approach.) As such they do not come boasting that they alone have the good of man and society in view. They cannot claim to have the answers. They want to stand at the side of those who seek the good and who administer the details. They offer their members to the larger society as participants equipped (in Christian intention) through a study of God's law to have care and to carefully minister to the need of the other. This modest approach is a denial of and a disappointment to the perfectionist who forgets that even in Christendom the Utopia of Christianopolis was denied.

The impotence of the churches today is particularly evident in their inability to speak clearly on the problems of war and peace in a nuclear age. Here is another instance where it is difficult to assign blame; it seems more necessary to report on the difficulty. The churches are silent, not always because they do not care but because the alternatives of tyranny and nuclear war are equally abhorrent and because in the nature of power structures today "nobody asked them." As years pass and the Cold War is better understood, the churches may find more effective ways to deal with this issue. Their complicated witness on the subject of human relations and race relations is improving as the displaced situation becomes more clear. "Placed" Christendom looks for the security of the ground it occupies; it segregates. The churches in it are captive to their local visions. In the ecumenical, international age and in the mobility and variety of contacts that the dialogical possibility opens, more and more the churches are beginning to rectify this narrowness of vision. Again, the concept of "displacement," just as it colored a theological premise, can be of help in understanding a sociological condition.

The third great ethical area—after peace and race—in those portions of the world that were once called Christendom has to do with the abundance and affluence of a technical society. (There is, of course, the opposite problem: that of the emergent and poor nations. But for the most part affluence appears in the nations of displaced Christendom: the British Isles, Western Germany and France, Scandinavia, North America, and a few colonies.)

The affluent society presents a complicated problem because in some respects it creates the illusions which blind Christians who are defensive over their place. On the other hand, it is the abundant society that brings about the reality of displacement. The technical features of such a society force mobility on persons. Its media of communication bring the whole world to each person. But, paradoxically, the economic abundance has made it possible for people to buy islands and masks. The move to the American suburbs was essentially a withdrawal from the urban intersectionality. Superhighways that take him through the city at high speed keep the suburbanite from actual direct contact with any single poor person. The world of advertising is geared to the white upper middle class and creates the illusion that the products it celebrates are available to men everywhere.

In the process the actual detail of personal life is forgotten: who envisions the political prisoner in Spain or Siberia; the American convict, the Moroccan refugee, the individual Chinese in an antheap culture; the slum dweller, the bloated, starving Indian child? To awaken the imagination to such realities Christian and secular leaders need to work together. Often the Christian voice can encourage the nation and the people in it to look beyond themselves. At other times, because the pattern of voluntary church life finds churches locating themselves chiefly in the islands of affluence, Christians may be the least imaginative about the needs of a hungry world. Sociologist Gerhard Lenski,[5] expert at studying the interplay between location and Christian attitudes, has uncovered urban situations in which church people were most protective of their own security, least understanding of the whole world's need, and least ready to extend foreign aid without the promise of political return.

The days of pure and simple Marxist interpretation of Christian life—"economy determines religion"—are passing as the result of studies by Lenski and others. The Weberian approach—that religion determines economics, in part—is coming into new currency. Plainly the problem now inheres in the narrowness of vision and in the weakness of the religious signals sent out by many churches. The situation of abundance represents something quite new to many Christians of the West. Life in a money world in which the majority of the people in a society are prosperous was not envisioned in most of Christian history.

The churches, making their way as voluntary associations in a secular world, are often imprisoned by the habits they acquire from sharing in the economic abundance. Their fund-raising methods, their dependence on their clientele's generosity (and prejudices), their own adoption of secular success standards, their own ability to manipulate men for purposes of campaigns and crusades—these have set them in a situation where judgment, then analysis, then patient listening are required. Here the recognition and reality of displacement must become a root experience of the churches if the ethical word is to be heard anew.

The breach between Christian and secular communities and the relative impotence of the church to be of help in the great ethical questions of the West (peace, race, affluence) have led to a further dismissal of the churches from the power centers and vital locations of decision. In most nations of the West one can discuss the nature of public character and morality and what to do about them without reference to the churches. The secularity which says one can get along whether or not one believes in God forces the inevitable conclusion that public character and morality are also sought independently of religious orientation. When the secular order does notice or does express an inadequacy, and does turn to the churches (their moral interest casts a longer shadow than their theological), a breakdown of communication occurs.

The churches do not customarily define themselves first as agents or instruments for producing public morality and national character. They seek first to witness to the jagged character of the revelation that shaped them: in the instance of the Christian churches this means that they define themselves first as redemptive fellowships that seek to serve the world. The churches that come to more and more realization of their displaced situation will be in a better position to expend their resources for the sake of the public good than will those concerned with keeping up appearances, drawing a space between themselves and the world around.

In American life, for instance, the Founding Fathers, bored by the theological claims of the individual churches, had a positive attitude toward the totality of the religious enterprise, but not for the interpretation of life churches might bring or for their hopes of heaven. They (Benjamin Franklin is typical) were interested in the morality churches could contribute toward the public good. This societal expectation was lived out most simply when the churches had a legal place (to about 1834 at the latest) or, later on, when they had fashioned a Protestant America. Then their suasion could produce laws effecting Protestant versions of morality. The *nomos* —or legal-based ethic—belonged to the era of Protestantdom. Its residues here and there place the churches in the position of pathetic retreaters in the public realm and as moralists in the ec-clesiastical.

In the more recent situation they have drawn on the other set of Christian resources: shaping character through accent on *agape,* the kind of divine love which spontaneously motivates man to serve others. *Nomos* ethics are operative in society only where the Law of God is believed in explicitly or where its incorporation in human laws can be coerced and enforced. *Agape* ethics must also be be-lieved; they call for inner disciplines and a greater imagination. But this ethic does have a power to transform and to motivate which coercion does not. Unfortunately, the love-oriented ethic easily descends into sentimentality or unconcern; this is part of the ethical problem in states with large Christian minorities.

The churches are, in the exposed situation, easily judged for their ethical inadequacies. When (as in America) two-thirds of a nation is nominally church-related, one can say: if you churches do your whole work with your own people, more than half of the nation's problem will be solved. (Christians have a somewhat different view of ethical potentials in the world of man, but they are not likely to make their point very easily and cannot wait for action until they do!) The fact that much of the Christian ethic is part of the hidden life, of working in self-disciplines, in quiet and loneliness, this hidden life is known to the Christian. But it passes by the point of empirical analysis with which the larger culture looks to the Christian church in a dialogic society.

Along with the hiddenness of personal ethics there are the parables of the Christian life which are located in situations of high efficiency in relation to the environment's energy resources. The lay academies of Western Europe, the ethical validity of the

Negro Christian leadership of the American South, the occasional strength of witness in an inner-city church—in all these areas public parables grow from Christian servanthood. Alas, their rarity and the appetite of the public media usually force them into an overexposure they cannot endure and point to the fragility of the best forms of Christian action.

What are the barriers against understanding? Some are theological. The low level of their Biblical literacy prevents many Christians from knowing in detail what it is to be called by the name of Jesus Christ. Baptism is followed by a life of cheap grace tinged with moralism. Sometimes theological literacy appeals to individualistic, spiritualistic concerns which abstract people from life. Another theological problem of recent decades was the ethical lapse following the demise of that serious theological liberalism which—at least in ethics—shamed much of orthodoxy and conservatism. The ethical resources in the more recent theological movements have not always been clear or clearly presented. At any rate, they are not part of the coinage of the great bulk of church people.

More frequently the problem is institutional—in other words, the fault lies in self-defensiveness over the loss of a Christian place. The self-seeking of competitive Christian institutions is hardly a winning ethical parable. The capitulation of church strategy to the ideological pattern of competitive free-enterprise systems hardly leaves the churches free to shape a different kind of character in this economic world. The questionable ethics of much religious fund-raising, public relations, and crowd manipulation is obvious to the larger community when the latter cares to look. The insistence on the church's exemptions and endowments and good name, where it exists, plainly runs counter to the Christian's self-emptying claim in the ethical realm.

Another cluster of problems is of a more practical kind. Protestant theology in particular has developed what has been called an "old maid" approach to public and political life. It holds to a purism that scorns those who get their hands dirty, who are really involved in the complex of human power. The divisions among Christians keep their impact from being felt. The tendency to generalize in preaching where the specific and concrete is called for has been a limiting factor. The reliance on the pulpit—a frail or false instrument for most political action—at the expense of the seminar, the academy, the movement, and the cell has limited Christians. The cult of personality and the quest for the "good man" have blinded them to the political good that the "semi-good man" may do. The newness of the secular church-state reality has confused others. The Christian's inability to use the public schools for religious character formation has bewildered those Protestants who once relied on them. The dependence of the churches on their constituents' financial support muffles prophecy ("You aren't prophetic about letting Negroes move into the community in the middle of a three-year financial drive").

The serious questioner can ask: Were you the arch-enemy of the good in the City of Man, and you wished to attack the agents of good, would you attack the churches? The question cannot be answered unambiguously, for the reasons of "hiddenness" and quiet work stated above. Even in the displaced situation, after exposure, we do not yet know what moral life and political conduct would look like entirely apart from Christian witness. The churches, displaced from the legal situation in which they could coerce obedience to their versions of morality, are now involved in interpreting a society and then producing for it: first, a man; then, an informed man; then, an involved man—a sojourner and stranger in the City, who cares for it and is careful in it.

Part Three

The Chance

for the

Church

8 THE CHURCH:

ECUMENICAL AND LOCAL

THE DISPLACED Christian who realizes the cultural and social dimensions of his new life must somewhere take a first step in witness and service. Our analysis to this point may have left two false impressions. All the talk about pilgrimage, exile, displacement, may have seemed to place the Christian alone in the world. Not nurtured by a permanent bond with his environment, too mobile to become well acquainted with others—shall he devise a lonely, personal Christianity apart from life in the church? Second: since the public picture of the church is in question, since massive forces and movements serve to displace the church, how shall it make its way? The first phase of our reply has necessarily dealt with the public life of the church. How does it walk in the world? In the attempt to deal with the church in the world of arts, sciences, media, politics, "church" may have seemed to refer to some sort of remote power elite.

Were this all that can be said, we could not blame a faithful church member if he feels left out. He may have identified himself as the displaced one. He may have joined the author in analyzing the masks, the illusions, the buffers, which the church as an institution employs to screen itself from the realities of displacement. But

127

when it came to countering the forces around him and to expressing himself, he may have felt excluded.

For many a faithful church member has no access to public life. He votes on the first Tuesday after the first Monday in November every couple of years. Once a year, through his service club, he sells peanuts for the sake of children. She serves her community through the P.T.A. They have a cousin in the Peace Corps. She "paints by number" on Sunday afternoons, and no gallery will ask her for Christian witness. His only contact with university life is a once-a-year payment of alumni dues. A disc jockey dedicated a record to them on their fifteenth wedding anniversary, but that is the only time they were related to the "sending" end of the media. He would not be elected dogcatcher if he ran for office.

He lays bricks for buildings. She washes diapers. He runs a farm. She punches a time clock. They send children to school. She freezes food for winter. He takes out hospital insurance. He works in a mine. She plays a cello. Their children watch television, like any others. They do not hope for too much in life: only some security, some ability to be of use to others. A summer vacation and a weekend away, a good laugh at the movies and the recovery of health, are enough. These are the planes where life is lived, where the realities of Christian displacement are becoming known, where few chances to reply seem open.

He and she are good faithful church members. They cannot personally take on themselves the full weight of a divided Christianity. They did not cause the denominations and would like to see pettiness in the church removed. They tithe, and are a bit uneasy about the pressure their congregation uses to motivate their more relaxed fellow members. When things are happening they are there: she teaches church school, he is a trustee. A neighboring church needs encouragement, and they will help. They read the denomination's magazines, are concerned with the mission of the church. Enormous reservoirs of goodwill, energy, generosity, they provide for the church. They may have problems of faith, but these may be less acute than their minister's. They may not be theologically informed, may not be given to profound ideas, but nothing else in their way of life demands profundity and little challenges them.

The reasonable prosperity of the times has affected them, and they can afford a house in a medium-cost suburb. The children have good air and healthy bodies and good schools. They are disciplined children and are generous and empathetic toward those in less fortunate circumstances. The sociologists and polltakers could find enough misunderstandings of the church in their responses and they would help complicate the graphs that analysts prepare. But in the world of jamming and competitive signals, against the background of the frailty of what it is to be a human, they are probably as faithful as their forefathers were. They form part of that hidden flock of Jesus Christ that is to be reckoned with until the end-time. Where do they fit in? Where do they belong? What can they do?

It is of the nature of church life in an age of social and cultural change that one cannot provide pat answers and simple programs to show the part they should play. All the books on how to administer parishes and devise clever promotions come much more easily from those who view the parish on diagrammatic lines. As they see it, there is a space to be cleared under the sun. There are the boundaries and there the preserves. There are the elites and bureaus. There is the method to keep the organization going. Enough of this programmatic material exists. The displaced Christian knows that the alternative is not another set of programmatic devices. He knows that to incorporate the responses that mobility evokes into precut plans denies the very thing that his time needs. But if he cannot be provided with a plan, he can be brought into discussion of the meaning of the church life in which, each week, he helps Christian response take form.

Thinking about the church in an age of displacement must begin with some sense of what we mean by church. This book is written on the premise that no sociological view of the church should be presented which is not theologically tenable. We have also suggested that much of the primitive Christian thought on the church, reproduced in the Bible, is more congenial to the dialogical, mobile, dynamic view of Christian life than to "ground-occupying," imperial Christianity. A way of viewing the meaning of the church in the Reformation period expresses well the theological background of this study. It is derived from the classic depiction of the church in Luther's comment (in his Large Catechism) on the Third Article of the Apostles' Creed.

There the sequence which gives birth to the church is described. The church is not established by the state (Christendom) nor formed as a voluntary association of like-minded people. The initiative for the church remains in God, is the action of the Holy Spirit. "He first leads us into his holy community, placing us upon the bosom of the church, where he preaches to us and brings us to Christ." This assertion amounts to a charter for the displaced life of the church. Christian life is not dependent on a certain accident of historical forms, on a form of institution tied to a particular moment. Rather, it exists wherever the Spirit of God moves among men, in any time.

In the face of the individualisms which isolate the exilic Christian, Luther asserts that the Holy Spirit works "through the Christian church" as his means. The church is not the accidental by-product of individual Christian life. It is the instrument of God's working. In distinction from the spiritualistic, abstract, and Docetic views of the church (a tempting alternative when the forces of the visible world displace the Church), the exposition insists on locating the church in the concrete order: "God has a unique community in the world."

The church is defined as the inevitable, not the arbitrary, corollary of the Spirit's work. The church "is the mother that begets and bears every Christian through the Word of God." Here is the protection against the idea of developing pseudo-churches alongside the real church. The need to develop special ministries and to reject many features which adhere to existing forms of the church tempts many to talk of abandoning life nurtured by Word, Sacrament, preaching, and fellowship and to "go underground" or out into the world of elites of power. The church is rather to be pictured as a feeding, nurturing mother in regular and constant relation to God's child.

The center of the church's proclamation is Jesus Christ: "For where Christ is not preached, there is no Holy Spirit to create, call, and gather the Christian church, and outside it no one can come to the Lord Christ." When sociology of religion becomes mere sociology of religion it cannot make sense of the hidden life in Christ.

Once again, against the individualisms, sectarianisms, abstractions, the character of the life in the church is made clear: "The word *ecclesia* means an assembly . . . a holy Christian people." They form a "community" under the Holy Spirit's agency. The church is shot through with interpersonality. The charts of church organization must deal with the "I-It"; for, as Buber reminds us, the "I-Thou" cannot be organized. The dynamism of church life is suggested in the assignment it is given; "The Holy Spirit carries on his work unceasingly until the last day. For this purpose he has appointed a community on earth, through which he speaks and does all his work. For he has not yet gathered together all his Christian people. . . ." The task of the church must be a base for the methods of its administration: "Therefore *everything* in the Christian church is so ordered that we may daily obtain full forgiveness of sins through the Word and through signs appointed to comfort and revive our consciences as long as we live."

Made up as the church is of sinners, its "exclusive" character dare never be sectarian or social; it dare not be based on clearing a space, creating a physical distance from the world. Its separation is theological: "Outside the Christian church [that is, where the Gospel is not] there is no forgiveness."[1]

This is the sum and substance of this phrase: I believe that there is on earth a little holy flock or community of pure saints under one head, Christ. It is called together by the Holy Spirit in one faith, mind, and understanding. It possesses a variety of gifts, yet is united in love without sect or schism. Of this community I also am a part and member, a participant and co-partner in all the blessings it possesses. I was brought to it by the Holy Spirit and incorporated into it through the fact that I have heard and still hear God's Word, which is the first step in entering it. Before we had advanced this far, we were entirely of the devil, knowing nothing of God and of Christ. Until the last day the Holy Spirit remains with the holy community or Christian people. Through it he gathers us, using it to teach and preach the Word. By it he creates and increases sanctification, causing it daily to grow and become strong in the faith and in the fruits of the Spirit.

Divine initiative, visible means, location in the world, constantly generating and regenerating, Christ-centered, personal, portable, disciplined: this Catholic view of the Church is shared by most elements of the classic Reformation. Anglicanism's similar view on these points is obvious. Nor did Calvinism reject the catholic view, as has been proven by J. S. Whale, among others.[2] The left-wing, anabaptist, and congregational emphases of the Reformation did stress much more the aspect of voluntary association. But the sociological weight of the whole original Protestant tradition opens it to the adaptive, concrete, mobile need of today. It was later experience—particularly the individualism of the eighteenth-century Enlightenment and the pietism of nineteenth-century Evangelicalism, or the static character of twentieth-century institutionalism—that obscured the dynamism.

No view of the church that is not thoroughly ecumenical—that is, oriented to the whole church in the whole world—will serve to relate the theology of the church to the age of the displaced Christian. In other ages the church was less constricted and the world less offended by division than it is today. In the context of this book, the roots of the ecumenical movement appear in the transition from a world that could be diagrammed to the dialogical world; from the sectioned space of Christian territorialism to the intersections of modern life.

Historically speaking, the nineteenth century occasioned the movement toward reunion in the twentieth. It is dangerous to judge the previous century in the light of today's needs. In the 1790s, when the great missionary movement to extend Christendom began, Christian division was less offensive. Only the United States was experiencing the beginnings of a realized pluralism. England had, of course, been long torn by the conflict between Anglicanism and the Puritan, separatist, and sectarian groups. But in an establishment, one group is licit and the others at best are tolerated. Only in the United States, with the rise of religious liberty, was there room for the parity that gave birth to open competition. That Scandinavia was Lutheran and Switzerland was Reformed was not such a scandal in a day of minimum interaction.

So from Germany and Scandinavia, from England and America, outposts of empire were extended. With the flag went the cross. In that age Christians occupied ground, received an empire, a place under the sun. They staked out a claim for the Norwegian Lutheran Church in India, the German or Dutch Reformed Church in Indonesia, the British Missionary Society in China, the American Baptist mission in the Pacific islands.

Only when the globe shrank, when transportation and communication brought people into contact with one another, did it become clear what had happened. The resurgent world religions looked unified in their territories; they asked questions and scorned Christians for their division. The modern political ideologies found Christian division useful to weaken religious resistance. Christians became aware of one another in new ways. So, around 1910, the first formal step leading toward what is now called the ecumenical movement was taken. The men who took the step had sensed the end of the opportunity of Christian imperialism that faced them.

The ecumenical movement can be misread or mislead, of course, as one more way of occupying ground for Christendom. But its reach to both sides of the Iron Curtain and both sides of the colonial-anticolonial tension, its hold in both affluent and depressed nations, guarantee it a contact with world reality that is a protection against provincialism, against "church tower history," which sees only the near at hand. Live contact with the many forms of ecumenical movement has provided twentieth-century Christians with one means of sustaining their imagination concerning the whole estate of the church in the world.

The ecumenical church, of course, is not a kind of power that will prevail on the world's terms either. Should the Protestant churches unite with one another and then with Orthodoxy, and should they both learn to speak a common language with Roman Catholicism—events not envisionable in the context of today's possibilities and open only to God who holds tomorrow's church in his hands—there still would not be the opportunity, or even necessarily the desire, for occupied ground, for a placed Christianity.

In the 1960s Christians might, in the scope of wildly inaccurate stabs at statistics, claim 28 per cent of world population. They would be twice as large a group as the next largest world religion. But such a feared "superchurch" would still be under the dominance of a "superworld." It would still be housed in nations whose ground rules are pluralistic for the most part. All the physical and psychic forces of the time guarantee that a uniting church will not be tempted, will not have the opportunity to dominate from its tall towers, as did its ancestors in Christendom.

The ecumenical church, eight hundred million strong, must be seen as "on earth a little holy flock or community of pure saints under one head, Christ . . . called together by the Holy Spirit in one faith, mind and understanding . . . [possessing] a variety of gifts, yet . . . united in love without sect or schism." Its essential life is hidden, though its effects are visible in the world. It may represent a mighty army (how confident were Christendom's missionary hymns about the way the banners and trumpets would overpower other worldly forces!) and yet, with the frailty of faith and the fragility of vision, it would hang onto the promise of God and life in the world as by a fingernail.

In this context the question of short-range or long-range strategies of the church's mission also enters. Frequently we are reminded that the antiecumenical forces—intransigent Pentecostal sects, extreme Fundamentalists, and others—are the most rapidly growing churches. The ecumenical churches are today more slow in statistical growth. Now, nothing should be said to ease the conscience of somnolent "ecumenical" people who limply suggest that it would be nice if the churches would all get together but themselves do not share in the churches' mission. And nothing should be said to disapprove the authentic motivation of sectarian Christians whose activity and quality of response often shame the settled heirs of a placed Christendom.

That is not the whole story. Something should be said of the dynamics involved. The missionary act is intersectional. It is not content with the size of the Christian place; it seeks to occupy more ground or it attempts to win people from alien ground. Its base may be heavily place-conscious. That is, missionary activity often works with the concepts of sending-centers, homelands, foreign territories, Christian lands, heathen lands. This mentality is disappearing as the missionary situation of the whole church in all the world is being perceived.

However, for all the wisdom that pentecostal and sectarian missionary activity can bring to the intersectioning of the church, the reuniting churches must take note of this: The church exists "by mission and for mission" but *not only* for them. It exists for salvation, for wholeness. It sends people back into life, and seeks to inform the common tasks. In its prayers and cares it takes responsibility for "all useful arts and sciences." The sectarian missionary separates himself from the strength of the whole church. He may neglect the less dramatic tasks of ministering and serving. His zeal, noble as it may be, often involves narrow views of the church and condemnation of the brother; sometimes it involves proselytism; some of its motivation comes from a prideful self-understanding: "only we have the truth." Meanwhile, the sectarian is trading off the labors and the goodwill which the less dramatic brother who is involved in other aspects of church life (such as recognizing union and working toward it) is effecting.

In short, the attempt to show that ecumenical churches are often less missionary and that more people will be saved if sectarian competition is unleashed falters on several points. It is a partial question: the church is to do many things besides adding to statistics. It involves a partial answer: the ecumenical churches are doing many things for God which the missionary sect may not be doing. What is needed is not a statistical comparison or a turning loose of competitive missionaries, but a supplementing and complementing of ecumenical and missionary strengths and burdens.

The ecumenical movement is not only the product of the age of displacement; it can further understanding by the mutual acceptance that it implies among churches. The security of my church's patterns of charity, worship, thinking about the faith, are creatively jostled by my observation of, and contact with, my brother whose church has different patterns. The jostling, disturbing as it may be to some ("What, learn *their* hymns?" "Bishops, for us? Never!" etc.), does open Christians to unenvisioned possibilities. The possibilities can take a responsible place within existing and known institutions. Christians can work with them and yet not be enslaved by them. They will not so easily again settle down to a cozy sense of place, "for the form of this world is passing away" (I Cor. 7:31) and Christians are to participate in it "as if not" participating. They take the existing forms of religious institutions (full of historical accident as they are) very seriously, but not too seriously.

The ecumenical movement stands in judgment on the Christian who measures the whole health of the church from his own tower. At the center of each believer's life should be the sense that if the Spirit of Christ is formed in others, he is one with them. Surrounding this reality is a necessity for confessing which in part divides. "Now I know in part" (I Cor. 13:12) but " we too believe, and so we speak" (II Cor. 4:13) RSV. One is not a Christian in general but a confessing Christian in particular. But the varieties of confessions are secondary to the ecumenical core. A third layer: the traditions of one's own church's concrete experience and memory are to be taken seriously. Interrupted as they may be, they provide the confessing Christian a base from which to view the world. They give color and texture to a specific faith which would be bleached and bland without them. To deny traditions is merely to make room for "manufactured rituals" to take their place. Traditions hold loyalties—even in the age of interruption and mobility. But they also divide. They must be judged by the confessional norm and the ecumenical core.

The fourth and outer layer is the denominational or organizational accident. A great portion of what a denomination is, is accident—of location, of culture, of language. Even more, the modern tendency to bureaucratize life and then seek legitimacies for this life demands the building of loyalties around denominations. Denominations are necessary as the present form of the concrete embodiment of church life. But they divide, and are to be judged by the cuticle of tradition, the necessity of confession, and the core of Christian unitive impulse.

In "placed" Christianity the layers are ordinarily seen and

judged from just the opposite direction. By far the greatest energy and loyalties are directed to the denomination and the energies it commands. Many of the organization's social and dramatic fictions are elevated to status of fact and regarded as ultimate truth. Then traditions are less understood, and confessions can be neglected and the ecumenical church denied. The reality of displacement and the concentration of Christian thought on the ecumenical problem could reverse in some measure this misdirection of loyalties.

From the world's viewpoint, denominational competition and self-seeking represent a low-efficiency yield on the environment's energy resources. The unredeemed world cannot care about the inner life of denominations unless they use this life to show their bearing and their bent to the world. If the doctrine of the church and the ecumenical reality are kept in mind, we can with less danger of provincialism focus on the entity most dismissed, most assaulted, most precariously defined in a displaced Christian's world: the local church in any specific place.

The local gathering (congregation, church, parish) bears the marks of the ecumenical church. Here most of all the Christian realizes that he is a "participant and co-partner" in the church's tasks and gifts. Here the unity of the church is asserted in hymn and prayer, sermon and intercession. Here men confess the name of Christ in the hearing of others. Here in the "little holy flock or community" one comes into living contact with at least some part of the flow of church traditions. Here, inevitably, in a technical society and a bureaucratic world, one comes into contact with the denominational accident—or with nondenominational surrogates which can be just as limited or limiting.

In the local church some sort of bond with the environment is fashioned. In Christendom this environment was a static, settled place where one lived and died in company with the same band of pilgrims. In displaced Christianity the environment represents a temporary, accidental bond with other sojourners. In a time of insecurity and change the sense of place is perhaps asserted more strongly than before. The local church in the act of providing the assets of concreteness in one place, often serves to imprison people against larger realities and view of other places. By providing a coherent view of an environment it may create illusions concerning the chaos of the larger environment. It may erect walls and barriers. It *may* provide a tower which one can climb to gain an impression of the health of the church.

In another book I once casually estimated that nine-tenths of all American Christians invest nine-tenths of their organized religious energies in the local parish. Numbers of critics have said this estimate is too low. The financial energies, the gathering of religious impressions, the outlets for the faith—most of them are directed to the local situation. In a parish of a thousand members, one delegate may go once a year to a church convention. Two out of one hundred dollars collected may go overseas. If the local preaching is dull, it is assumed by the congregation that preaching as such is always dull. If the local choir's *Te Deum* is shaky, the whole church's song is considered to be in poor condition. If the local church shows a glimpse of unity, the church in the world is considered to be loving. Thus Christians' impressions are gathered; once again, the process is full of illusions.

The local church also complicates the public picture of the faith. Undisciplined, uninformed "religious" symbols as opposed to Christian symbols are constantly being picked up out of the air. The sacred notions which the mass media propagate constantly are being received on believers' antennae. The church's public portrait is constantly being generalized about, without a basis in specific analysis or without concentrated imagination extended toward the whole church. So captive of place may the local church be that service-minded Christians avoid it, in order to be free for informed and disciplined life beyond it.

With all the interest in, and criticism of, the local parish, it is important to define it with care. Here the romanticism associated with Christian place must be scrutinized. Nostalgia for the settled normal parish, the church-tower point of view, yearning for the diagrammed life of the past—these can be limiting and enslaving visions today. Pseudo-churches developed by critical Christians alongside the real church can easily be made up of prideful elites. They can become cliques. They can be removed to the point of abstraction from the messy and loving realities which the local church in its quiet rhythms is called to represent.

If romanticism is dispelled, the local church can still stand on its own. While much of the present reality of the parish is a social fiction, an historical accident (whose justifiers find points of Biblical basis for it), the stress on visible, local embodiments of discipleship is clearly Biblical. What is needed is a theology of the parish which will serve the local church best by defining it most modestly, more humbly. Robert Frost has called a poem only a "momentary stay against confusion." I would say that a parish is only a momentary bond with an environment, a center where the Christian self can be organized in relation to other selves for the sake of serving the church and the whole world. All one church can do is momentarily to push back the pressures of confusion. In that context, with the public relational stress and all self-advertisement gone, the local parish is more free to live its true life. Most of that life is, like all life, made up of quiet drama and prose. An offense occurs when too much is expected of the local church, and its trivia must be made to appear tremendous and significant.

The Christian parish—a small idea, a trivial reality in the modern world. Yet it provides a place where people can keep their feet on the ground and derive strength. The local church can be seen as a microcosm, a miniature reproduction of the whole church. Christ is present. His Holy Spirit guides. The means of grace are here. People present to one another parables and opportunities. The plan of God is recapitulated, resumed in the rhythms of the local church's life. Here the "officially unimportant people" gather. The local parish is not capable of solving the whole (or even the larger part) of the socio-cultural problem of displaced Christianity. But it can keep itself out of the way of those who are working to solve the problem. It can equip people with resources to understand and to participate in the life of the whole church.

In the United States the term "parish" has interestingly gained much wider acceptance in recent years than it had in the past. It belongs to Anglican thought and represents settlement, the locating, and placing of the church in a geographical setting, in fourth-to seventh-century England. Today the term most frequently seems to be reached for to describe a local setting as a center of resistance to mobility and change. The "parish" minister delights in the fact that, in a chaotic universe, he is given responsibility for a particular plot of ground, a numbered and known group of people, a definable mission, a place.

The currency of the term bespeaks some of the kind of nostalgia that real-estate developers exploit. They flatten out land, pave it, bulldoze the trees, rubber stamp houses, and then call the development "estates," "fields," "meadows," "knolls," "groves." Modernity erodes the meaning of place, removes shelter, takes away static and definable life. Nostalgia evokes the words which create illusions of static place. To the modern parson, "parish" is one of these.

It is not likely that at this date anyone will undercut the term. If it is therapeutic to learn to live with ailments when they cannot be cured, we may learn to live with "parish." Etymologically and historically it meant just the opposite of what nostalgia takes it to mean. "Parish" came from *paroikein* and referred, in the second-century writings of Ignatius, Clement, and others, to the parishes or sojourning colonies of Christians on the move in various cities. Placed Christendom took and transformed a term of displacement.

If the parish is seen dynamically as a temporary bond with a fluid environment, it can serve a mission. If it is seen in the nostalgic sense: as defining a place, occupied ground—it can be the charter for irresponsibility concerning the whole church's life. The greatest danger for the parish today—a danger enhanced by the parish's advertisement and institutional aggrandizement—is its ecological imprisonment. Ecology refers to the locating of plants (or people). Ecology can see people imprisoned in the accidents of their temporary location. It can see barriers erected against people's understanding the world's need. The impression is often given that if the local church meets its annual visible goals (the budget, a building program), the whole church in the world will be healthy. It is possible, however, that the success of the local enterprise merely complicates the whole church's mission. The local church may add to the competition and self-advertisement, the misexpenditure of funds and energies. Its successes may increase the difficulty prosperous Christians have in empathizing with others who do not share their own setting. Ecological imprisonment afflicts most of all the churches in the affluent and suburban settings. These provide the last islands of illusion for many in the displaced world.

The local parish, institutionalized and placed, has been seen as the center of "four-wheel" Christendom. People are brought there in baby carriages for baptism, in limousines for marriage, in hearses for burial. Church is relegated to the private and familial, relaxed and leisured, portions of life. This relegation can distort the understanding of the public role of the church. Again: would the enemy of the good do well to center his attack against the placed parish?

The faults do not lie primarily in the theological intention of the local parish. They lie in the sociological temptations open to the local church as an institution, as a loyalty center. The temptations cannot easily be resisted by competitive denominations. With the kind of law which dictates a maximum convergence on areas of minimum need, they crowd churches together where they are least needed and desert the very areas where more people concentrate. The virtually instantaneous obsolescence of the products of expensive, located, fortress-obsessed Christianity has not yet burdened the consciences of many church-extension strategists.

Yet the local churches exist, full of illusion as they may be. Shall they be deserted and kept on as luxuries, recalling a conservative tradition of history? Shall they be deliberately killed off, along with other complicating fossils of the age of Christendom? Unlike the merely cultural artifacts associated with the church, which might be killed or allowed to die so that the displaced Christian would be really free, the parish represents a theological reality. The local church is people. The people exist. Were there only one man of faith in each local church, this would itself be the kind of miracle that warrants a ministry. Moreover, the local churches have responded to the kind of criticism I have been alluding to. They cannot "jump out of their skin"; they can-

not be submerged to give room to ill-defined pseudo-churches
ministering to elites. They exist and will exist. They demand and
deserve a word of judgment and grace where they are. Social
critics sometimes censure them for ideological fault when they
may be guilty only of nurturing the illusions "place" can give.
Critics often attribute to malice what should be attributed to
lethargy. Perhaps it is the critics who bring too high a view, too
high an expectation, to the parish!

Much can be done to equip the parish for life in the mobile
setting. As we said above, each parish can learn habits of thought
and word which will keep it from complicating the church at the
places of experiment or depression. Each can help counter the
hypercongregationalism which caters to local loyalties in selfish
fashion. Each can by tremendous and sustained acts of will devise
ways to escape ecological imprisonment. Otherwise, their statistical
successes may well continue; but they might gain their own souls
and lose the whole world.

The local church does not exist for its own sake but for the
"world" which is represented in the assaulted, interrupted, mobile
life of its own community. To the Christian, existing for the other
means mission and service. To determine that mission requires
an understanding of community in the displacing age. We cannot
here describe in detail the meaning of urbanism, suburbanism, or
rural life in today's world. We can glance only at some mechanisms for looking at community life after Christendom.

In Christendom, the local church assumed a dimensional reference to the environment. It towered over the local community.
It was lord of surrounding space, and it determined in part the
laws, arts, sciences, even of those in that place who did not
actively respond to its ministry. It could operate with *nomos* or
law and could carry out its sanctions through excommunication,
interdict, penance.

In the world after Christendom a different view of community
was born. The community, in the Wesleyan view, was now alienated. "The world is my parish," said John Wesley, whose followers
went out into the chaotic and disintegrative community to seek
and save souls and spread scriptural holiness. The community

they found had begun to have a secular assumption at its base, though appeals based on nostalgia still were effective. This "Wesleyan" relation to community holds to this day in modern mass evangelism. Mass evangelists often work in urban centers and appeal to the residue of "rural" (i.e., Christianity nurtured by sheltered space) culture.

To speak of "community" in a pluralistic society is in some senses a contradiction in terms. The pluralist society shares only ground rules ("Any number can play") and a minimum of creative but ill-defined ideology ("We hold these truths to be self-evident"). In the pluralism of the modern community the local church represents one voice among others. It has no dimensional, overtowering reference that is recognized by the outsider. It has only a substantive reference. What does it have to say and do? With what measure of efficiency does it bring its heart and its powers to bear on the energy resource of the environment?

The church contents itself with ministering to aspects of community. In a technical society the local congregations usually work with people who are dislocated from the place where most public decision occurs. They are far from the centers of power where their potential clients themselves hold some part in power collectives. They deal with the leisured portions of life. They see their mission undercut by the competition of other voices. The community is bombarded by mass media with signals from without and opened from within by gatekeepers to the larger pluralistic world.

The modern community is not a "natural" community; it did not just grow,[3] but was manufactured along economic or class lines. It is not an "historical" community; people do not remain in one place long enough to grow roots. Ordinarily it is not an intellectual community; the barbarian is to be found in its midst. It may be a religious community, but the religious assumptions must be—in the pluralist setting—so broad and vague as to be quasi-secular. This is the community of the age of displacement.

That Christians can try to locate in isolated environments where pluralism is not realized is, of course, true. But the urbanization of the modern world, the vast preponderance of people in the pluralist urban setting, limits this move as a strategy for the church.

Where the local church recognizes the complex nature of modern community it must do as the church in public life must. It must relate itself to a different set of energy resources. It will not merely snatch people out of the world and think its mission complete when they sign up on the dotted line for church membership. It will not exploit the goodwill of the community, will not advertise or come with a commercial hand outstretched. It will not stress competition or institutional power. Here on the local plane most of all it again must come to serve.

The creative local church carries on its mission to the community for the community's sake. It serves for intrinsic reasons. Its actions are more often pre-evangelical. As time passes opportunities will usually grow for overt evangelism, verbal contact. This sequence—beginning with intrinsic service, following with pre-evangelical contact, and only then making the verbal approach— reverses the right sequence in the eyes of many. Does it amount to "being ashamed of the offense of the Gospel"? No; rather, with ingenuity, it seeks to locate the actual offense of the Gospel in the new setting. It provides a sound approach to the real centers of the community and not just to the religiously preconditioned, the nice safe people who want the church to remove them from responsibility.

If in earlier parts of this book we spoke in terms of the responsibility of socially involved and culture-building people, this discussion of the local church inevitably focuses on the local minister. Theologically he may see himself as a professional layman (*laos:* the people of God). But sociologically he assumes a different role. In a technical society there is great curiosity about vocation. What do you do? What is your occupation? Who runs the organization? This kind of society lays extra burdens on the minister of the local church.

In placed Christendom a different situation obtained. Often the minister towered dimensionally: he was the civilized man, the only educated man in the community (which was coextensive with the parish). He was perhaps one of the few "occupational gate-keepers" to the larger world. He represented a universal church with (ordinarily) remote headquarters. He was the custodian of one portion of the mosaic of Christendom's places. He was this portion's center. He held certain charismatic and sacramental sanctions. Apart from his competence he was respected for certain religious powers. People came to him.

The parson of the era after Christendom bears a different relation to his environment. He now must relate himself to it substantively. There are other educated and able people: what does he have to say and do here? He is not alone among the gatekeepers: the community is constantly directed by outside signals. The universal character of the church is hardly recognized in the pluralism of almost any community: localism and congregationalism prevail in the competitive center. He is often regarded as the caretaker of an obsolete society, the guardian of a place which each year must yield ground. He moves in the modern world as belonging to it and yet often with different apparel, a different tone of voice. He must assert his competence as preacher, administrator, counselor; where church life is voluntary people can "shop" elsewhere (the term is even used). He must seek a gathering of people.

The setting of displacement is incarnated, then, in the professional layman who is the ordained clergyman. We must consider his role because he is a weathervane, a barometer of the church's condition and setting. The minister is caught between belief and unbelief, between truth and error, between a sense of mission accomplished and bad conscience for omission. Nervous, allergic, endocrine disorders characterize his body; nervous breakdown and even suicide, we are told, regularly occur. All these problems lead ministers to give a great deal of time to self-appraisal, possibly even to a kind of narcissism. "Admirals and clergymen . . . spend too much time commiserating with each other and totting up the special tribulations of the profession," complains literary critic Richard Chase.[4]

Here we shall avoid this obsession with self by a steadfast focusing on everything *but* the psychological burden of the ministry. Our interest is in its social role. The minister as technical and vocational "head" of the local church—no matter what the polity that sanctions him—personally represents the institution. The industrial and business society calls other men away from the parish

during the hours of the working day. The minister and the matri-
archy are left to work together. Where a masculine voice is called
for, he is counted upon to be there. He is much involved in the
world's crossroads. He is at home in divorce court and hospital. If
he has a conscience he may well be picketing or representing his
people in situations of need. Pick up the newspapers of the early
1960s (but not those of the religious revival of the 1950s!) in the
United States. In almost any story on, or photograph of, social
issues which gather people—issues of race, labor-management,
housing, neighborhood planning—the minister can be spotted. He
is there not because he is the only one in the parish who cares.
He may be alone on occasion, because his technical interest demands his being informed about certain types of issues on which
others do not take attitudes. As a more mobile representative of a
universal vision, he should be less "located" and self-preservative
than are many of the unordained laity in other vocations. But quite
often only he can make himself available in these socially concerned settings at the times of day when they occur. (I am not at
this point describing the minister whose only interest is defending the status quo, the religious "place." *Is* he a minister?)

The role of this kind of clergyman is ambiguous and complicated. In a sense this complicatedness results from diffuse definition. His main task is to make himself obsolete: he delights to
work "for the equipment of the saints for the work of ministry"
(Eph. 4:12) and is frustrated at the instinctive clericalism (in some
anticlerical societies too) that demands a professional person to fill
a role. Nor is he only the occupant of an ill-defined position ("What
does he do, if other laymen can also do what he does?"); he is
the "man in the middle" between societal expectations (diagrammatic: they assign him a place) and the theological vision (dialogical: it gives him a function and a mission).

The cultural expectation can be enslaving. Inside the church
and around it a cultural "place" is assigned him. Because of man's
instinctive uneasiness with the theological interruption, people
make the attempt to locate him. In this mind, he must be unin-
volved. He must not preach politics. He must not get his hands
dirty. He must suppress his opinions. He must not "throw his

weight around" because the institution he represents—unlike labor unions or teachers' guilds—has a transcendent reference. Its real life is in a heavenly commonwealth and its earthly life dare not complicate that vision. He should not be too involved. He should stay out of business and ethics.

I should add that recent studies have shown that these stereotypes of cultural distance are no longer universal. Disturbances in politics, ethics, and business have here and there led to the emergence of a kind of secular leader who asks for a certain kind of spiritual leader to promote dialogue. Some studies reveal businessmen complaining (contrary to the usual picture) that the church is not enough involved, not listening enough *or* offering enough counsel.

Still, it is safe to say that <u>the culture which allows any kind of place for religion and tradition likes to have the church around, likes to have a minister around</u>. It seeks some sort of sanction for its actions, some sort of baptism of its rites, some sort of soothing of its anxieties. <u>The minister is needed and then dismissed as a caretaker of the museum of religious tradition</u>. The portrait of the minister in the mass media (unless he happens to be the hero) is of interest here. Casually introduced, he usually stands around at the edges of life's celebrations. He is the ritualist at initiation, puberty, fertility, and burial rites. When he speaks he uses a kind of voice no one else uses. He never has anything really important to say. The vitalities of the plot move beyond and around him. <u>He is the aging, silver-haired, mellifluous, and unctuous fossil.</u>

In this cultural expectation, he is trapped because of his inner vision. On the one hand, he knows himself to be much more involved than the world recognizes. He may well be aware of his own sin, frailty, ignorance, and doubt—and may wish to reach out to others as their kin on this basis. He does not like to be a monument or a rock of faith. He knows that he sees much more of the world than many around him do, and his interpretation of it may be more sophisticated than theirs by theology and worldly opinion. But even more, he is aware of the theological necessity laid upon him. <u>He is to be responsible for a group of Christ's holy people</u>—so he dare not create too great a social distance between himself and them. Yet he must not be the slave of cultural expectations. If he does yield too much to what is expected, he cannot speak the prophetic word and be at the side of the worldling in need.

He must shatter the cultural expectation and yet he cannot resort to devices, mannerisms, or spectacularities which draw attention to his person (e.g., the beatnik's beard, the uncouth way of the rebel). Meanwhile, he is upstaged by other spokesmen for the spiritual life who have access to the media of expression. There is theological validity and practical necessity behind his work, but he is caught in a cultural bind. The Roman Catholic Ecumenical Council of the 1960s reflects this kind of concern among the bishops. They are charged with responsibility in an area of the church. Yet the public derives its knowledge of Catholicism from the press releases and public statements of nonepiscopal spokesmen. The Council of 1870, by separating qualitatively the claims of one bishop, removed some of the charism the others all need. The Protestant clergy might also profit from an ecumenical council that would define their situation.

Programmatic solutions are secondary: give the minister more salary, a better house, a better pension—so he can be a better professional. Give him exemptions and status. Let him afford a psychiatrist. All these streamlining devices, including the idea of assigning his routine tasks to the unordained, may be helpful to him personally. They may also further clutter the cultural expectation! Conceptual changes concerning the ministry are more salutary. H. Richard Niebuhr's suggestion that the clergyman see himself as "pastoral director"[5] of the parish has surprising New Testament warrant, but represents a still unsatisfying peace with destiny. It helps define and organize, but it does not help solve the question of misplaced cultural expectations.

The usual therapy suggested is, as we noted, programmatic. Or it may involve external adjustments to modernity: linguistic or sartorial change. What is needed, I believe, is a changed self-conception on the part of the clergyman that will force a revision of every cultural expectation in every move he makes. He must show (*parson* meant representative person) that he most of all knows the meaning of displacement and dislocation. He must embody aspects of the solution. He must be most aware of the revolutionary world. Yes, he must be responsible in relation to the prose of his parish. But he is to brush his parish constantly against the Curtains of ideology, rescue it from fanaticisms, face the world's nihilisms, interpret its power, be at home in its dynamisms. None of these roles will necessarily cure his allergies, ulcers, or nerves. But it will keep him too occupied to notice them so much.

The suggestion which follows is perverse on the surface. A slight misreading of it could distort my intention and make it meaningless. What should a minister *be* in order to change the cultural expectation, reveal his true interest, and be free to serve?

He must be the theologian. Theologian: the worker with the strange task of relating the Word of God to the world of man. He is the scandalous occupant of an offensive vocation: to speak of the unspeakable and to relate himself to the world as one most at home with the finite. "I am no theologian!" many a parson will protest. If he knows what he is saying, he is to be pitied. He is like a white-suited scalpel-wielder who, just before the ether is administered, bends over the patient and says, "Now, I am no surgeon, but . . ."

The protesting parson says he is no theologian because he is not, and he need not be, one particular kind of theologian. He is not an academic theologian. He is not a technical analyst or synthesizer. He is not abstracted from the church's concern. But theology is something other than abstraction. Where does its representative belong in the concrete world? Any minister can perform a simple experiment. Next time someone casually asks him what he does, let him answer that he is a parish minister. Let him time himself to see how long the questioning will be sustained on that line. What denomination? How big a congregation? Where? Then curiosity fades. The next time drop the offensive term: "I am a theologian, ministering to a congregation." When (and if?) communication resumes he will find himself defining, explaining, relating—and finding opportunities to correct all kinds of captivating cultural misconceptions. Little curiosity is brought to the parish minister as custodian of a nonvital location of culture. But the embarrassment that meets someone who tries to relate Word of God to world of man provides a different opening. How often does a parish minister—including one of high degree—awaken national interest? Yet professional theologians are quite frequently the objects of interest for their interpretation of life.

Cultural expectations are low when related to placed Christianity, when settled in the mores. Goodwill, it is true, is extended, but not "ears to hear." The priest, the rabbi, are seen to be sufficiently strangers, sufficiently the disinherited to have something to say (though many of them are serenely located in actuality). The Protestant minister needs their kind of social distance in order to draw attention to the environment.

The question comes to him, "What do you do?" He sees death second to the undertaker, divorce second to the lawyer, counseling second to the psychiatrist, administration second to the executive, teaching second to the teacher, disease second to the physician. A technical society asks, "What do you do? What are you first-best at?" He studies, relates, and enacts the drama of Word and world. This answer, it is true, jostles his cultural place. It should.

Until he makes that answer he is seen as a self-protective institutionalist.[6] The studies of Protestant congregations reveal that even their lay leadership often sees these enclaves first as institutions (ineffective policing agencies and fund-raising centers); second as instruments (they build morality, like the Brownies); third as representatives in their ideologies of idea patterns in a syncretist environment ("Well, they are all true; Presbyterianism is just the line he was born into and is pushing"); fourth, as social conclaves; only fifth—in small minority—as redemptive fellowships. What is more, lay leaders think that in this sequence they are reproducing what the minister wants them to reproduce. They have noticed where his time and energy and his most emphatic words go.

There is no simple solution to this problem. The only effective answer is the hardest: reversal of the usual conception of the minister's role by a determined effort to cancel the pictures of the minister as cultural custodian, administrator, "good joe." This requires a tremendous act of will—which is a stroke for the freedom to educate. Surveys find that ministers rank teaching low on their list of activities. They administer first, counsel second, serve as preacher and priest third, and teach last. Shouldn't they be told: When in cultural difficulty, study and teach; press the weakest point and make it strongest.

This means that the minister should devise more formal teaching opportunities (that would probably be as ill-attended as the few present ones are), and also that he should "exploit" his every contact with his people and with the community: he should be a teaching preacher. (The Sunday noon response "That was an inspiring sermon" is less likely to issue in piety or action than "I never thought of it that way before!") He would be a teaching administrator, a teaching counselor, who kept constantly in view the purpose of the church and not merely the purpose of a program in a changing world.

Some catalytic reference is necessary for his self-understanding, and I should like to propose one. Just as I do not seriously suggest that the term "theologian" enter into parlance constantly to characterize his enterprise—ordinarily it belongs to his inner world— so I shall suggest a term that is sufficiently unusable to prevent its being seen as a programmatic device. The clerical or lay reader of this book could let this interpretation become part of his consciousness even though he found the term cumbersome. Try it: let the minister think of himself as a *catechist*. He may pick some other term if he chooses, but at least the colors of "catechist" commend it for self-interpretation:

The minister wants to change a cultural expectation and open the door for a world-changing word. As a certain kind of teacher he can set up a momentary stay against confusion. If education is a "conscious and willed selection of the effective world" (Buber), he consciously and deliberately selects to interpret his role as a catechist.

First, his task should include some aspects of the etymology. To begin with, *kateecheo* means "to resound into the ear of, to make believable." The term bears a rich patina of memories and connotations. Paul wrote that he would rather speak one meaningful word (he uses this term) than speak a thousand in tongues. The cultural custodian, from the viewpoint of a dynamic culture around him, speaks in tongues. He uses strange tones of voice, hallowed and remote images, spiritualistic and obsolete terms, to guard his cultural space. The catechist knows that faith comes by hearing, that voice is a summons to belief. He stakes his integrity on what he is to say: "This is what makes me act; give it a chance."

Second, the catechist refers not only to his belief but to a substance outside himself—a revelation, a witness. It is the church's teaching that he utters and not just a weekly transfer of the teleology of his own moral experience. This fact extricates him from narcissism: if the unexamined life isn't *worth* living, the overexamined life *isn't* living. Catechesis permits the minister to look beyond the subjective to the objective.

The word has an archaic ring. It recalls the church of the earliest centuries, when the primitive disciple in a displacing world was called into life for the end-time. Further, it has a sacramental connotation. Cathechists prepared people for baptism and the Lord's Supper, for the central rites and rhythms of the church's life in an alien world. Catechesis was connected with the call to discipleship, with the test of devotion, with the understanding of faith's uprooting center. The word also has a missionary ring. Where is the catechist used by the church today? Where the church's resources run out: one village further into the jungle, one crossroads further out in the plain. Catechists remind the churches that in a missionary situation the whole church is at the edge of its resources. Again, the term recalls the Reformation. At decisive turns in its life the church produces enchiridions, catechisms, to translate the central ideas for a mobile populace. (Needless to say, this catechetical task is not to be equated with the mere reproduction of historic catechisms, though the church today could learn from them. Nor am I speaking of rote memory or of answering questions that are not being asked. Here I refer to method and self-understanding alone.)

Finally—though much more could be said—catechetical teaching relates to a coherence. Out of the chaos of a universe, experience is distilled and concentrated, brought to memorable order. The literary form criticism of the Gospels shows how the evangelists organized, selected, gathered, and reproduced materials to enforce a point (John 20:31, etc., or the first verses of Luke). There is a liturgical or catechetical ring to much of the formal teaching in the New Testament epistles. The maieutic Greeks and the rabbis taught this way. What occurs? The teacher who brings this kind of coherence helps organize the signals of a displacing world without distorting them.

What about the nonprofessional, unordained layman? Practically all of what was said above applies to him if he is in a position of leadership. We hear much today of the revival of the laity; most of it has been directed inward, on the life of the church. We have not yet seen enough of catechists or enactors who bring their vision to the world. So often, unfortunately, laymen are exploited so that they can mime the cleric's world, be judged by his standards. This exploitation accounts, no doubt, for the fact that the yield from the environment's resources is often higher the further the layman is removed from his local parish (which wants to use him) and the closer he is to the institutes or retreats and academies. He is handicapped by the Catholic definition of the church on clerical lines and the general Protestant lack of definition. He is able to give the church only his leisure hours, his second-best time. Were it possible better to measure and report on the "hidden laity," the underground of ethical and verbal witness beyond church auspices, it would be easier to define its role apart from the clerical rubber stamp.

What does a layman do? In the technical world he does not do all the things the ordained man does—not because of technical incompetence but for the sake of definition. In most rites baptizing a child is not technically complicated, but the complex society looks to the professional to do it. (I am aware that in some churches the validity of baptism is questioned if it is administered by the noncleric.) What does a layman do? He helps the professional. He is, the programmers advise, to relieve the minister of routine administration. In the process he is relegated to secondary status. He does more of the same routine he has engaged in all day and his other talents are unchallenged. What does he do? He does what the clergyman does, but does it less well.

The unordained laity will best come into its own in a teaching church. The layman will not be asked to give up his vocation to become a clergyman. He will be equipped to serve where the church's resources give out; his training must be "portable" for he is mobile. He cannot be equipped just for safe location on the organizational chart of one congregation. The question of his beliefs and their nature must be called into question: Does he really believe? Can he become a disciple? (Not: How can be be a better churchman?)

The institutionalization of the church is what most of all affects and imprisons him. The minister at least has time in the variety of his week to deal with the jarring and jagged excitement of the theological venture. The layman often is asked to see the church only in its securities, in its administrative strengths.

Some breakthroughs in the understanding of laity have occurred. The World Council of Churches Department of the Laity is of help. The lay academies of Europe and America and the catechetical schools in missionary ventures are models.[7] Iona, Sigtuna, Parishfield, Taizé, the Kirchentag—rubrically, one can recite the location of ventures. One may look to them with hope and still see their limits. They cannot displace the less dramatic parochial ventures.

The breakthroughs usually come where the really displaced character of the faith is discovered: in post-Christian Europe, in laboring and religiously "burnt-over" areas. The situations are parables more than patterns. One must deal with the laity where it is, and it is difficult to dramatize the serious attention of the church to the layman in the typical parish. He cannot immediately be uprooted for so dramatic a remedy. Radical experiments usually demand charismatic leaders of the kind the seminary or parish does not develop. They demand communitarian patterns of living which are not open to most adult laymen and laywomen, who rarely can take the time off to live apart. It is often hard to communicate their experiences in the humdrum of the parish; they have developed a language of their own and their experience is at too great variance from local church expectations.

Experiment in the parish must parallel continuing work in the centers of concentration and advantage. Partnership is important. The lay academic witnesses to the displacement of the world. He calls his brother in the settled, located parish to a vision of the world's real need. Each needs the other to understand revolution in the church, to empathize with it, and—if it becomes necessary in their respective settings—to share in it.

9 THE NURTURE OF THE
DISPLACED CHRISTIAN

THE PORTRAIT of worldly, exposed Christianity that
has been drawn on these pages is in danger of being misread. To
some it will appear that such a release of the church's prerogatives, such an unconcern over its place as I advocate, would lead to
the depletion of all churchly resources. The church would always
be spending and not taking in. It would always be serving and
never being strengthened. It would live its whole life in the world
and would never withdraw to be nourished. It would be so in
touch with the concrete that it would not allow for an interrupting word from the infinite. It would be so busy that it could
not worship, so practical that it would be ugly, so undisciplined
and reckless that it would be anarchic. But none of these is necessary or desirable in the church of a disinheriting generation envisioned here. What of nurture and sustenance? What does personal
life in the church look like in this vision?

My views on this line may look quite conservative and apparently contradictory, for they appear in a traditional mold. They
represent an attempt to relate a catholic, classic, coherent Christianity to a changing world. They appear in polar contrast to the
exposed life of the displaced Christian.

156

How is the displaced Christian nurtured? The traditional means are all employed: contemplation and meditation, prayer and intercession, reading of the Bible and of Christian literature, witness, conversation, burden-bearing, the sacramental life of the church. One could cite others. Any of them could be stretched to full-length illustration. Rather than merely cite each, I should like to dwell on the most obvious form: nurturing the displaced Christian through preaching. Analogies could be drawn from this one central act for the other traditional modes.

Why preaching? Most attempts at Christian apology include a great deal of advertising. One gets the impression at the beginning that in this book or that the question of the ages will be solved. One will somehow find himself eliding into the realm of the knowledge of God. Even in an unbelieving or a religious world, somehow the scandal of the Gospel is at last going to be smoothed out, the paradox relaxed, the bumps leveled over. Along the way many an author can do much to clear away the debris, the barriers, the hurdles. But at a certain point he suddenly comes to a position where, if he wants to present a faith recognizably Christian, he shifts the terms. He is free, of course, to present natural philosophy or humanist ethics and call it Christian. He is also free to draw a short-legged, thick-skinned, tusked animal and call it a giraffe. The problem is that he is talking about something other than the Christian faith or giraffes to those of us who have seen either.

If Christian apology discusses the classic catholic faith, sooner or later it lays its cards on the table. Eventually it refers to God's unexpected, historical answer in Jesus Christ. Eventually it deals with the characteristic mode of awakening faith in him and nurturing the believer: "Faith cometh by hearing." Mine has not been a book of apology; it has been interested in the socio-cultural setting of the faith. So we begin the question of nurture where the apologist would end it: faith cometh by hearing.

Somehow, along with the acts of love and silent witness, the parables and paradigms, the displaced Christian comes to this point: God's revelation occurs in places, lands, races, times, events, people, persons, prophets, a Person. These are open to him in part through a written record, a product of the ancient world. But the Christian faith, while it allows for the birth of faith and its nurture among the deaf, also knows the importance of oral representation of the Word. Somewhere, in some sort of verbal action that we are here terming preaching, the Word is spoken, preached, taught, sung, cajoled, incanted, insinuated. In preaching, the living Word is recognized and Christ is present. Something happens—in the liturgy, says the Christian; it does not *not* happen. That makes all the difference. It means that preaching is not just to consist in words about God. That would be like reading to a hungry man out of the cookbook, says Kierkegaard. It is offering the hungry man an apple in outstretched hand, says a modern definition. It is one hungry man telling another where to find food, says another. In any case, reading is nurturing and feeding in a living context.

So far, so good. "Now show to us that this happens," says the questioner. Most of the empirical data is on his side: our culture produces many sermons and large audiences, but seldom is preaching an event, an excitement. Seldom does it relate to the revolutionary world, to the realities of displacement. Should it? Can it? Why the interest in preaching?

The Christian cannot easily get away from verbal witness. He knows that the Biblical *kēēryxon ton logon,* preach the Word, is a mandate, a command, not a temporary injunction or a recommendation. It is not revoked because the cultural context grows complex. Of course, the command should not be strait-jacketed into the routine of 11:00 A.M. pew-and-pulpit Christianity. That stereotype dominates talk of preaching. (Even motion picture producers line up the polite Palestinians who respond on the screen as if a bell had rung, walking with the joyless decorum of suburbanites and assuming seats as if the offering had just been taken, to hear the first Sermon on the Mount.) Sermons occur everywhere. Some campus pastors abandon the pulpit for the corridors. It takes no courage to say "I am not ashamed of the Gospel" before a mass audience. It does take courage to say it before the other person in a dormitory hall.

The Christian is commanded to preach. Preaching is a virtually universal activity of the churches. Not all churches stress the sacraments, but the sacramental churches are all open to preaching. As a "foolishness" (in St. Paul's term), preaching is an indicator or a measure of how the whole Christian enterprise is faring. It is a nearly normative activity: many churchgoers measure the health of the whole church by the strength of the preaching in their local church.

Preaching is overburdened in an overworded world. Recommendations come at people from all directions. Advertisers, columnists, harlequins, hucksters, demagogues—all have verbal advice. Everyone knows more, has more to say. How can the preached word make its way in such a culture? Finally, preaching is a time-consuming activity of the church and its leaders. This most common activity of evangelical Christianity—what is its condition?

Faith, says Luther, is "an acoustical affair." It is a sacrament of sound waves. Whenever preaching occurs an event is involved, from the viewpoint of faith. From the viewpoint of culture the issue is more complicated. What kind of event does it become? What is this generation's problem in the matter of having "ears to hear"? Every age, we have asserted, has a theological problem. Is the theological problem always complicated by the culture of the time? Unfortunately, in the curious snobbery of clericalism, we have few studies of the audiences and settings of preaching. We have libraries full of forgettable sermon books, shelves full of books on the preacher and preaching. Assume that the audience outnumbers the preacher: who notices it? Yet in an age of reckoning, counting, interviewing, poll-taking it should be possible more frequently to find out what is being heard.

Culturally, this is not a great age for preaching. Christendom knew a romantic age of preaching when the minister towered over the congregation. In Santayana's terms once more, that age was picturesque and passionate and sometimes unhappy. Its passing may be a catastrophe but is no reason for despair. Unfortunately, some preaching and listening are still modeled on that age.

What has taken the romantic age's place? When renewal is mentioned in the church we hear of the ecumenical movement, lay

activity, evangelism, Biblical theology, stewardship. Few are
ready to add "renewal of preaching" to this list and then to document it. The Princes of the Pulpit who, two generations ago,
strutted their stuff across great stages in churches built to accom-
modate their style, have few successors and will have fewer. (We
are convinced, however, that the craft of preaching in the multi-
tude of pulpits has improved since the day when the advertised
orator raised false expectations, developed local mimics, and
wearied lesser known proclaimers.) Few names of preachers are
known by the man on the street as they were known in the romantic
age of preaching. Few sermons make news; when they do it is
usually because of their relation to a contemporary event (the
Blake-Pike proposal; calls for racial integration) which possessed a
separate newsmaking dynamism. Ministers themselves bring low
expectations to preaching: a sermon, says Bishop Gerald Kennedy,
is something a minister will go across the country to deliver but
will not cross the street to hear. Ministers know that a brief letter
to a magazine editor will stir up more discussion among their
colleagues and their people than would the same substance in
sermonic form. Few sermon books are memorable; ask a publisher
to try to remember what his list of such books was two seasons
ago! Few people in our culture look to preaching with high expectations. Perhaps it is time to revise the definitions of intention
and to see preaching in a different context.

We shall use three architectural models to describe the times
and modes of the church's life and relate preaching and worship to
them. Each is directly related to the problem of the displaced
Christian and can illustrate the other modes of nurture and
expression.

First, worship and preaching occur in the cave (as opposed to
the lecture hall); that is, they are liturgical and not moralistic, if
they wish to counter the cultural expectations of today.

Second, worship and preaching occur in the tent (as opposed to
the fortress); that is, they are edifying and informing and not institu-
tionally self-seeking, if they wish to counter cultural preconcep-
tions.

Third, worship and preaching occur in the city (as opposed to the island); that is, they are concrete and world-oriented and not self-preservative and abstracted from life.

These characteristics are not self-contraditory. Sometimes they are in tension in a tripolar arrangement. At other times they appear in chronological sequence. At still other times one dominates over the other. The "catechetical" minister prepares the ground for these definitions. (By no means are these exhaustive or precise terms; they are characteristic and not prescribed patterns.)

Nurturing in the cave: the cave represents a primitive architectural form. The cave has figured, Stephen Hirzel reminds us,[1] in all theoretical treatises and in many actual buildings of recent years. It foregoes the niceties of placed Christianity's buildings, which sought to embellish and decorate an empire. It represents the church withdrawn, disciplined, inhaling, adoring, retreating. It refutes the cultural expectation that the church exists only to moralize. Alec Vidler, after a visit to America two decades ago, wrote an article on the "appalling moralism" of the pulpit.[2] He heard dozens of sermons and then said he could reduce their rhetoric to one phrase: May I recommend to you that you try to be good? This phrase sums up the method of the institutional lecture hall, which removes all element of transcendence or surprise. Preaching along these lines is expectable and nonmemorable.

But to ask the church to constrict itself before it enlarges, to have a vision before it shares one, to drink deep and eat well before it acts—this is a surprising demand. Does it contradict our emphasis on "enworlding the evangel"? Not at all—if it seems to, we have misstated the alternative. Even in the act of adoring, the world is remembered, but now it is used and transformed: "Good men use the world in order to enjoy God, whereas bad men want to use God in order to enjoy the world" (Augustine). The homily of adoration as opposed to the platitudinous pep-talk uses the raw materials of human experience—bread, wine, water, a book; a laugh, a tear; stained glass and clay and candlelight—and uses them to return the song of praise to God.

The church exists for God's sake; hence the first word is theological, in the cave. The church exists for its own sake; hence the second word is for equipping, in the tent. The church exists for the world; hence the third word implies service in the city.

For God's sake: sight, sound, underground, the church turned inward. Seen by itself that activity looks like Freudian withdrawal, ethical evasion, sociological huddling, hiding, lapsing into aestheticism (the great "cave church"—Le Corbusier's Pilgrimage Chapel at Ronchamps, France—has been accused of appealing to all these interests by those who deny the full rhythm of the church). But liturgical preaching begins in the cave and uses the concreteness of the experience: "Taste and see that the Lord is sweet." Often Protestant theology says there are no holy places because all are holy. But the liturgical Christian who agrees (in the matter of ethics) knows that in the revelatory constellation there are places where holiness is intensified. The liturgical Christian receives something he would not have received had he not shared in the event of adoration.

The cave makes man restless. It is unfamiliar; it locates his unbelief, his rootlessness, the subjectivity of his religiousness. But it also provides an opportunity for the Word. "A presence is never mute" (Teilhard). Now man may be spoken to in the setting of verbal incarnation, as if he had not heard before. Definition portrays the legitimacy of the venture; it frees the conscience of the church which always feels it must be "doing something." Earthy, concrete, historical, personal—this characterizes the substance of which liturgical service is born, from which it is transformed. It wallows in the weakness of God so that his strength may be recognized in the glorified wounds. The cave is the narrow passage to the broad street.

The tent. By itself as a permanent situation the cave is selfish and evasive. The church moves into the broader passage. Again, as Hirzel reminds us, architectural treatises and actual buildings today recall the tent for Christians. Not only economics and mobility, the external dictations and practical need, but also the inner understandings of time, space, and deity commend the tent. It is the perfect model for the equipment of the displaced Christian. He is the sojourner, the exile, the wanderer, the alien. He is part of the people of God temporarily gathered from the world in the church for the world.

The tent is posed not against cave and city but between them; it is posed against the fortress. Building for eternity was characteristic of the bastions and tall towers of total Christendom. The persistent fortress image suggests romance, nostalgia—witness the Gothic revival in the United States in the very years when displacement of Christendom was becoming part of consciousness. The most liberal preachers built the most impressive Gothic fortresses to share the romance, to gain strength from an imagined past whose myth, not whose faith, they shared.

In the tent the nurturer is not a scold but an understanding person; he is not the huckster or the monument builder, but the motive leader. For an hour the flock of Jesus Christ is made temporarily visible, gathered. The Old Testament tabernacle is recalled. God is with us. The New Testament: the Word was made flesh and tented among us. We have here no continuing city.

The fortress builds its own walls, is a self-directed enterprise. (The churchgoer should think what percentage of the sermons he has heard have gone to building up the institution without reference to the reasons for the existence of the institution. That is what we mean by "cultural expectations.") For "fortress preaching" the minister dismisses the rhetoric of religion, steps down into the aisle, and asserts the church's prestige—in order to make the budget, keep tax exemption, subsidize the tall towers. No hint of self-emptying there.

The fortress shuts out the world. The sermon then distorts, builds the illusions in which obsolete "placed" Christianity thrives. It shuts out people from the world, directing their best energies to erecting the stone piles instead of serving in the City of Man.

The church worshiping and preaching in the symbolism of the tent recalls the world around (the city) and the vision within (the cave). It knows the transitoriness and the nomadism which occasions the tent. It seeks the tragic sense of life that copes with such a setting. It seeks not to complicate the lives of those whose tents are pitched nearer the battlegrounds and crossroads that day. It seeks to inculcate the common vision of the eternal city and the real temporality open to the pilgrim who is not insecure about keeping his promised "place." It points to the common interests and needs of the whole world; it is not concerned with the status of its own location in the world. It listens through the thin walls for the language of today's world, so that the language of Canaan can be related to it. It recalls and retells in new forms the story that precedes faith. It has modest intentions and simple methods. It empathizes with the nomads; it is directed to their need. "Love is a foreign language; all men mispronounce it," says Christopher Morley. The sermon is a lesson in diction and an act of love.

Finally, there is the city, and in the city there is the test. The church has inhaled; now it exhales. It withdrew; now it attacks. The cathedral is overtowered by the skyscrapers in the modern city; so, no longer, will the tall towers of romantic Christendom prevail. The church bears a substantive, not a dimensional, reference to the city. It must have something to say and a way to live. Here the effects of catechesis, teaching, liturgical and edifying preaching, will be tested. A sermon should not be preached in a church but in the city, said Luther in a church. Kierkegaard said: Take Luther up on it; move out into the city.

Such preaching does not imply a mere external adaptation of language, architecture, and garb. It means taking the mask off the spiritual word and off the city. It means understanding, judging, and loving. The church as it moves out into the city to minister does not just ask what will the city yield to it, but how rather the church can expend itself on the City of Man even if there be no return on the investment.

Words stop. The displaced Christian is alone, in the city. The world's powers seem to care little about his faith; they have a mild interest in its tired, quaint cultural forms. Their vitalities express other curiosities. But the Christian has been sustained once more. What holds together his personal life? He asks questions, legitimate questions, of the future of faith. Does the breakdown of Christendom mean the breakdown of the Christian faith? That word "still": can one *still* believe, can one *still* profitably invest his hopes in the church, lost and rooted in places and no longer remembered? That word "still" is the canker in the fruit, the malignancy in the marrow. The Christian takes some comfort from the fact that Jesus himself expressed such thought: "When the Son of man comes, will he find faith on earth?" (Luke 18:8). He has profited from definition: he can separate the churches' sociological agony from their theological agony; but he still has his personal agony.

The displaced Christian is not regularly permitted to hold the romantic view of the past (though he may enjoy it on occasion). He cannot bind himself to the nonvital elements he would find congenial in the culture of the present. He asks about the future of faith. He is surrounded by churchmen who suggest that faith is theologically easy to come by and sustain, if it is at ease in the culture. He hears recollections of the days when it must have been easier to believe. He knows the fragility of his own faith in any kind of setting.

Once more he returns to the matrix. Before he deserts the revelation extended to him: has he really heard it and taken it seriously? Gods there be many and lords there be many—has he taken seriously the *one* Lord who reaches out to him (I Cor. 8:5-6)? He takes courage from the Psalms: God has decisively turned toward him. Christ has revealed the Fatherly heart. But his imagination cannot long sustain these ideas. What would God do if he, man, died (Rilke)? He, like Abraham, is called to go out. He did not even know the realities of his displacement until he took the faith seriously. Will he share Abraham's experience? Would it not be better to return to the illusions of shelter, and to stay there? Should he join those who try to occupy ground for the faith and climb the tall towers? Shall bravado, bandwagons, keeping up appearances, whistling in the dark, substitute for the quiet hour of his dark night?

The best he can do is to notice that the Bible pictures anxiety over the future of faith because of the untrustworthiness not of God but of man; not because God will revoke his promise but because man will be faithless. He finds that Christian action vivifies the promise and makes it more possible for him to have ears to hear the next time the promise is extended. He takes seriously the mandates of God and the presence of his neighbor. He sees Jesus Christ who "for the joy that was set before him endured the cross" (Heb. 12:2), and first draws near when he hears a cry with which he can identify: "My God, my God, why hast thou forsaken me?" (Matt. 27:46).

He hears, as he follows, that discipleship calls him to "a lover's quarrel with the world."[3] He is given a task instead of a place, a relation instead of an empire. He is called to watch one hour and sees how Christ calls him to his own side. He hears of the agony of Christ until the end of time, and resolves not to be caught asleep. He is called to the vision of the glory, also in the middle of the world. He is asked not to worry about the future of faith: faith *is* future. Faith is again possible in the midst of the very world which displaces him. Not easy, but possible.

These all died in faith, not having received what was promised, but having seen it and greeted it from afar, and having acknowledged that they were strangers and exiles on the earth. For people who speak thus make it clear that they are seeking a homeland. If they had been think- ing of that land from which they had gone out, they would have had opportunity to return. But as it is, they desire a better country, that is, a heavenly one. Therefore God is not ashamed to be called their God, for he has prepared for them a city. . . .

Let brotherly love continue. Do not neglect to show hospitality to strangers. . . .   (Heb. 11:13-16; 13:1-2)

NOTES

CHAPTER 1

1. The Christian Church is an Imperial power—"not a mere creed or philosophy but a *counter kingdom*." "It occupied ground; it claimed to rule over those whom hitherto this world's governments ruled over without rival; and it is only in proportion as things that are brought into this kingdom and made subservient to it; it is only as kings and princes, nobles and rulers, men of business and men of letters, the craftsman and the trader and the labourer humble themselves to Christ's Church and (in the language of the prophet Isaiah) 'bow down to her with their faces toward the earth and lick up the dust of her feet,' that the world becomes living and spiritual, and a fit object of love and a resting-place for Christians." "The Communion of Saints," in *Parochial Sermons* (1st ed.), IV, p. 201.
2. George Santayana, *Character and Opinion in the United States* (Originally published in 1920. New York: Doubleday, 1956), p. vi.
3. Thus St. Clement begins the Epistle to the Corinthians: "The Church of God which sojourneth in Rome to the Church of God which sojourneth in Corinth . . ." and see especially The Epistle to Diognetus.
4. See Joseph Warren Beach, *Obsessive Images* (Minneapolis: University of Minnesota, 1960), especially chaps. 17-20.

CHAPTER 2

1. Christopher Dawson, *The Historic Reality of Christian Culture* (New York: Harper, 1960), p. 43.
2. Efforts continue into the present; the history up to 1950 is recounted in Anson Phelps Stokes, *Church and the State in the United States* (New York: Harper, 1950), Vol. III, pp. 582-91.

CHAPTER 3

1. Walter J. Ong, S.J., develops the distinction somewhat overoptimistically, I believe, in "The Religious-Secular Dialogue," in *Religion in America* (New York: Meridian, 1958), pp. 170 ff.

2. Based on the statistics of the Population Branch of the United Nations, a projection "if present rates of increase continue unchecked." Reproduced in graphic form in *Horizon*, Sept., 1958, Vol. I, No.1, pp. 54-55.
3. For example, Gabriel Vahanian, *The Death of God* (New York: Braziller, 1961).
4. Eugene Rolfe, *The Intelligent Agnostic's Introduction to Christianity* (London: Skeffington, 1959), p. 19.
5. Retold on the basis of Franz Kafka, "The Hunger Artist," in *The Penal Colony* (New York: Schocken, 1948), pp. 231 ff.

CHAPTER 4

1. A consistent theme in the writings of Troeltsch, it is focused in Ernst Troeltsch, *Christian Thought: Its History and Application* (New York: Meridian, 1957), p. 177.

CHAPTER 5

1. See Winthrop Hudson, *American Protestantism* (Chicago: University of Chicago, 1961), chap. 2.
2. H. Richard Niebuhr, *The Kingdom of God in America* (New York: Harper, 1937), p. 17.
3. John Kenneth Galbraith, *The Liberal Hour* (Boston: Houghton, Mifflin, 1960), pp. 79 ff.
4. Peter Berger, *The Noise of Solemn Assemblies* (New York: Doubleday, 1961), p. 11.
5. See Franklin L. Baumer, *Religion and the Rise of Skepticism* (New York: Harcourt, Brace, 1960), pp. 230 ff.; J. Paul Williams, *What Americans Believe and How They Worship* (rev. ed., New York: Harper, 1962), pp. 472 ff.; and Deane Ferm, "The Road Ahead in Religion," in *The Christian Century*, LXXVII, p. 636, and "The Road Ahead in the Church," in *The Christian Century*, LXXVIII, p. 1426.

CHAPTER 6

1. One of these examples in Alexander Miller, *The Man in the Mirror* (New York: Doubleday, 1958), p. 15.
2.   Jede dumpfe Umkehr der Welt hat solche Enterbte,
         denen das Frühere nicht und noch nicht das Nächste gehört.
Quoted in Erich Heller, *The Disinherited Mind* (New York: Farrar, Straus and Company, 1952), title page. Heller's translation of Rilke's "Seventh Elegy."

3. Joachim de Fiore (1132-1202 *ca.*), a mystic who envisioned a third dispensation of history belonging to the Holy Spirit.

4. Oral tradition, at St. Andrew's Scotland Faith and Order Meeting of the World Council of Churches, Summer, 1960.

5. In John Gossner, [ed.] *Best American Plays 1945-51* (New York: Crown, 1952), p. 33.

6. Christopher Dawson, *Religion and Culture* (New York: Sheed & Ward, 1948), p. 201.

7. In Christopher Fry, *Three Plays* (New York: Oxford Hesperides, 1961), p. 209.

8. See "The Violent Tenor of Life," the first chapter in J. Huizinga, *The Waning of the Middle Ages* (New York: Doubleday, 1954).

9. From an essay, "Theology in the University," in *Radical Monotheism and Western Culture* (New York: Harper, 1960), pp. 93 ff.

10. This "thermodynamic" view of change and culture is a running argument based on Marshall D. Sahlins and Elman R. Service, *Evolution and Culture* (Ann Arbor: University of Michigan, 1960), pp. 75, 4, 7, *23*, 48, 73, *82*, *97*, 105, 99; the italicized page numbers are the more important citations.

CHAPTER 7

1. From the *Letters* of Gustave Flaubert, quoted in Carl Michalson, *The Hinge of History* (New York: Scribner's, 1959), p. 19.

2. The conversation is summarized in John Chapman (ed.), *Best Plays of 1950-51* (New York: Dodd, Mead, 1951), p. 94.

3. Quoted in "Forms of Human Community," in Rudolf Bultmann, *Essays* (New York: Macmillan, 1955), p. 300.

4. In *The Improper Opinion* (Philadelphia: Westminster, 1961).

5. Reported on in studies of Detroit area Lutherans in an unpublished survey in 1962; for a complete approach to the Detroit correlations of religion and political-economic attitudes see Gerhard Lenski, *The Religious Factor* (New York: Doubleday, 1961).

CHAPTER 8

1. *The Large Catechism of Martin Luther,* translated by Robert H. Fischer (Philadelphia: Muhlenberg, 1959), pp. 59 ff.

2. J. S. Whale, *Christian Doctrine* (London: Collins, 1957), pp. 140 ff.

3. See the essay, "Forms of Human Community," in Rudolf Bultmann, *Essays* (New York: Macmillan, 1955), pp. 291 ff.

4. Richard Chase, *The Democratic Vista* (New York: Doubleday, 1958), p. 24.

5. H. Richard Niebuhr, *The Purpose of the Church and Its Ministry* (New York: Harper, 1956), pp. 79 ff.
6. Roy W. Fairchild and John Charles Wynn, *Families in the Church: A Protestant Survey* (New York: Association Press, 1961), pp. 167 ff.
7. See Margaret Frakes, *Bridges to Understanding* (Philadelphia: Muhlenberg, 1960), pp. 125 ff.

CHAPTER 9

1. Stephen Hirzel in *The Christian Century,* Feb. 19, 1958.
2. Quoted by Donald Coggan, in *Stewards of Grace* (London: Hodder & Stoughton, 1958), p. 44.
3. Robert Frost suggests his own epitaph in *Collected Poems of Robert Frost* (Garden City: Halcyon House, 1942), p. 451.

INDEX

Format by Sidney Feinberg
Set in Linotype Times Roman
Composed, printed and bound by The Haddon Craftsmen, Inc.
HARPER & ROW, PUBLISHERS, INCORPORATED